A STATUE FOR AMERICA

THE FIRST 100 YEARS OF THE STATUE OF LIBERTY

by Jonathan Harris

FOUR WINDS PRESS
Macmillan Publishing Company
New York

Macmillan books are available at special discounts
for bulk purchases for sales promotions, premiums,
fund raising, or educational use. Special editions
or book excerpts can also be created to specification.
For details, contact:

Special Sales Director
Macmillan Publishing Company
866 Third Avenue
New York, N.Y. 10022

Macmillan Publishing Company
866 Third Avenue, New York, NY 10022
Collier Macmillan Canada, Inc.

Printed in the United States of America

10 9 8 7 6 5 4 3 2 1

The text of this book is set in 11 pt. Aster.
The illustrations are black and white photographs
reproduced in halftone.

Library of Congress Cataloging-in-Publication Data
Harris, Jonathan.
A statue for America.
Bibliography: p.
Includes index.
Summary: Gives the history of the first one hundred
years of the statue standing as an international symbol of freedom.
1. Statue of Liberty National Monument (New York, N.Y.)
—History—Juvenile literature. 2. Statue of Liberty
(New York, N.Y.)—History—Juvenile literature.
[1. Statue of Liberty (New York, N.Y.) 2. National
monuments. 3. Statues] I. Title.
F128.64.I6H36 1985 974.7'1 85-42808
ISBN 0-02-742730-7

ACKNOWLEDGMENTS

More individuals contributed indispensable assistance to the creation of this book than can be listed here. Librarians who helped guide the author through the numerous collections include Won Kim of the Statue of Liberty National Monument; Jennifer Bright of the Museum of the City of New York; Bara Levin, archivist-historian at Chemical Bank; and Elizabeth Raskopf of the New-York Historical Society. At the New York Public Library, the staff of the Rare Books and Manuscripts Division, the Local History Division, the Picture Collection, the Newspaper Annex, and the Office of Special Collections were unfailingly cooperative.

Bill Gaines and Anne Griffiths devoted an evening to a delightful interview and a special tour of their unique collection of Statue models and memorabilia.

Sheila McCauley of the Liberty Centennial Student Campaign, youth branch of the Statue of Liberty-Ellis Island Foundation, furnished abundant materials and much useful information.

A brief Author's Query in the *New York Times Book Review* yielded a rich harvest of responses from persons in many parts of the U.S., who offered reminiscences and special knowledge of the Statue. Again, only a partial (alphabetical) listing is possible: Francis Czachorowski, Torrington, Conn.; Justin Crum, Roslyn Heights, N.Y.; Blossom Esainko, New York City; Paul J. Harris, West Hartford, Conn.; Seth D. Harris, Houston, Tex.; David Kraus, Rockville Centre, N.Y.; Rev. James F. Kuntz, Principal, Saint Peter's Prep, Jersey City, N.J.; E. Manneck, Clarence, N.Y.; Evelyn Phillips, Director of Publications, Roslyn Public Schools, Roslyn, N.Y.; N. Polinsky, Robert W. Carbonara School, Valley Stream, N.Y.; Thomas J. Smith, Jr., Galveston, Tex.; Mrs. Ronald A. Weiss, Ellisville, Mo.; Mrs. Chilton Williamson, West Townshend, Vt.; and George P. Williamson, Shrewsbury, N.J.

Patricia Fieldsteel helped arrange the personal and business connections that made this book possible, and alerted the author to recent developments affecting the Statue.

Endlessly supportive and prolific with creative suggestions as always was my wife, Martha Harris.

To my mother, Becky,
first lady in my family
to be welcomed by
the Lady

CONTENTS

A STATUE
⋆ FOR ⋆
AMERICA

· 1 ·
BIRTH OF THE LADY

Colossal statuary . . . ought to produce an emotion in the breast of the spectator.
— Frédéric Auguste Bartholdi,
sculptor of the Statue of Liberty, 1885

The young French sculptor stood before the giant statues of the Pharaohs and the ancient gods and goddesses of Egypt. His name was Frédéric Auguste Bartholdi. This was his first journey through Egypt. It was an experience that shaped his entire career. In those timeless sculptures, he had recognized his own destiny.

For thousands of years these huge stone carvings had loomed over the desert sands, inspiring awe in all who beheld them. Bartholdi promised himself that he too would create monuments of towering size.

His sculptures would be designed, as he wrote later, to "produce an emotion in the breast of the spectator." They would do this not only because of their size. Each gigantic work would move the viewer "because its size is in keeping with the idea that it interprets, and with the place which it will occupy."

There has never been a better description of Bartholdi's masterpiece, the Statue of Liberty.

Bartholdi had been brought up in a well-respected, highly educated Alsatian family. His father was a prominent public official. The family lived in comfortable circumstances until 1836, when Bartholdi's father suddenly died. Frédéric was then only two years old. His strong-willed mother faced the task of raising him and his brother single-handedly.

Frédéric's father had expressed the hope that the boy would study law, and then take up a career of public service. But the young Bartholdi soon found that he preferred art. Mme. Bartholdi granted the boy's wish, and saw to it that he obtained the finest training then available.

Bartholdi was just eighteen when he received his first public commission. His hometown of Colmar assigned him to create a statue of one of its native sons, who had risen to become a general in Napoleon's army. When the resulting work was unveiled four years later, in 1856, its impressive size and dynamic style immediately made Bartholdi's reputation.

The unveiling of his first major sculpture coincided with Bartholdi's first trip to Egypt. Over the next decade, he produced a series of heroic-sized monuments which graced the public squares of several French cities. He even had to have a special fifteen-foot door cut through the wall of his Paris studio, so that his enormous statues could be moved in and out—sometimes in sections.

One evening in the summer of 1865, Bartholdi was

Bartholdi in his Paris studio. One of his earliest models of the Statue stands at his left.

invited to dine at a house in a little town just outside Versailles. His host, a distinguished law professor and historian named Edouard René Lefebvre de Laboulaye, was also his friend and patron. Laboulaye had commissioned Bartholdi to produce a bust of him. The other guests were equally eminent in politics and literature.

The after-dinner conversation turned to the question of whether any nation ever truly appreciated help received from another. Someone cited the case of America. France, the speaker pointed out, had sent her ships and soldiers to aid in the great war for American independence. Yet France could not count on America's gratitude.

Laboulaye vigorously denied this. He was a long-time admirer of the United States and its democratic system of government. He had written a three-volume history of the United States and had lectured widely on the American Constitution.

"The American Nation," Laboulaye now insisted, "has more sympathy for France than for any other European nation." The shared sufferings and triumphs of the American Revolution were not forgotten: "When hearts have beaten together, something always remains." This was as true "among nations as among individuals."

The esteem of Laboulaye and other French liberals for the United States had been heightened by the recently concluded Civil War. In their eyes, that bloody struggle had proved once again America's willingness to sacrifice for the cause of liberty.

Laboulaye's feelings on this subject were especially strong. A kindly but determined idealist, he was a founder and had long been chairman of the French antislavery society. It was an issue on which he would never compromise.

In 1862, at a time when the outcome of the Civil War was still very much in doubt, Laboulaye had written a pamphlet eloquently defending and explaining the Union cause to the people of France. "Frenchmen," he wrote, "who have not forgotten Lafayette nor the glorious memories we left behind in the New World, it is your cause which is on trial in the United States." Only by supporting the Union could France "hold aloft with a firm hand the old French banner, on which is inscribed Liberty."

The American ambassador to France, John Bigelow, was so impressed by Laboulaye's manifesto that he sent copies of it to government leaders and diplomats all over Europe. One copy went to William Cullen Bryant, widely respected author, poet, and editor of the *New York Evening Post*. Bryant had the document translated into English, published it in his newspaper, and had it distributed throughout the North.

A shrewd judge of politics, Laboulaye knew that the outcome of the American Civil War would have far-reaching effects on the political situation in other countries. He wrote to Bigelow that if the Union were defeated, the enemies of democracy all over Europe would rejoice. They would claim the war's outcome had proved once and for all

> that no republic can withstand the shock of civil or foreign war, that the people cannot rule themselves and are made to be led by lords, soldiers and officials, and that their welfare lies in obedience, their freedom in submission.

For Frenchmen of that era, there was some risk in holding and expressing views that favored government by the people. Their government was then rigidly controlled by the dictator, Emperor Napoleon III. He sternly disapproved of any talk of freedom and democracy. Anyone who expressed such thoughts was in danger of arrest and imprisonment.

One way to get around the restrictions was by writing and talking about struggles for freedom in faraway places. Government censors rarely took action against such discussions as long as they seemed to imply no direct criticism of the emperor or his regime. America, revered by French liberals as the great bastion of democracy, was a favorite subject. Intelligent readers could easily make their own connections.

Some dared to disagree in more direct ways. At least one all-French unit fought as part of the Union army. The French colony in New York had turned out a regiment of volunteers. It became the 55th New York Infantry, which distinguished itself in battle though it suffered heavy losses. There were French officers in other units as well, even including two royal princes.

Then, in April 1865, came the assassination of Abraham Lincoln. Few events in American history have ever stirred the French so deeply. It produced a spontaneous outpouring of sympathy from French citizens of every class and every walk of life.

A collection was taken up nationwide for a medal expressing the people's sympathy for Mrs. Lincoln. To ensure that it truly represented the common people's sentiments, no more than two sous was accepted from any contributor.

A young journalist presented the medal to the American ambassador. "Tell Mrs. Lincoln," the young man said, "that in this little box is the heart of France."

Events and memories such as these underlay the conversation that evening at Professor Laboulaye's dinner. America was very much on Frenchmen's minds in those days—especially Frenchmen like Laboulaye's guests, who yearned for the establishment in their own country of a democratic society like that which flourished in America.

Laboulaye reminded his guests that America would soon be celebrating the hundredth anniversary of her Revolution. "If a monument should rise in the United States, as a memorial to their independence, I should think it only natural if it were built by united effort—a common work of both our nations."

An inspired notion, though Laboulaye had spoken it only as a passing thought. He had no specific plan in mind; he probably forgot the whole idea almost as soon as he mentioned it.

Bartholdi could not forget it. A monument to American independence and freedom, to be built by the peoples of both nations—now that was an idea to set fire to a sculptor's imagination!

But the time was not ripe for a monument embodying the concept of revolution. Under Napoleon's repressive government, such ideas were regarded as treason. Few Frenchmen would risk publicly supporting a project that might be considered a challenge to the emperor's rule.

Bartholdi never entirely abandoned his dream. From time to time, for his own inner satisfaction, he experimented with small clay models. He kept trying to work out the right image for a monument honoring the struggle for American independence.

Meanwhile, Bartholdi considered other projects. In 1869, he paid a second visit to Egypt. The occasion was the opening of the Suez Canal, which had been built by French engineers and financed almost entirely by French investors. Fascinated as always by the possibilities of the colossal in sculpture, Bartholdi conceived the idea of a huge statue at the entrance to the canal.

It would take the form of a stately female *fellah,* an Egyptian peasant, robed in the ancient style and holding a torch aloft. The statue could thus serve as a lighthouse, as well as a tribute to the idea of "Egypt Carrying the Light to Asia." Bartholdi's plan called for it to reach a height of more than ninety-two feet from base to torch, atop a pedestal almost fifty feet high. It would have ranked among the world's tallest statues.

Bartholdi broached his idea to Ismail Pasha, the khedive, or ruler, of Egypt. The sculptor probably reminded the khedive that this would not be the first monument of its kind. A famous precedent had existed in ancient times: the Colossus of Rhodes. This was a bronze statue of the sun god, Helios, reputedly over one hundred feet high, which once had guarded the entrance to the harbor on the Greek island of Rhodes. It too held up a torch to light the way for arriving and departing vessels. An earthquake toppled the mighty structure in 224 B.C.

Ismail Pasha seemed to favor Bartholdi's idea, and the sculptor made a few small test models. But the highly changeable Ismail soon lost interest, and the project had to be abandoned. Bartholdi's sketches and models are all that remain of it today.

The following year, Bartholdi's career was interrupted when Napoleon III embroiled France in war with Prussia. The patriotic sculptor volunteered for military service at once.

Commissioned a major, he was sent to organize and command a local force of militia in Colmar, which was close to the Prussian border. Bartholdi was able to muster only a pathetically small force. When the Prussian battalions moved forward, he and his outnumbered militiamen could only retreat. Later in the war he participated in several battles, but the cause proved hopeless.

The war resulted in a swift and crushing defeat for Napoleon III. Captured by the enemy and thoroughly humiliated, the emperor had no choice but to give up the throne and go into exile.

The Prussians imposed harsh peace terms. They annexed two provinces of France, Lorraine and Alsace. They forced the French to pay a huge indemnity of five billion francs. A Prussian army of occupation remained on French soil for two years, until the entire sum was paid.

The Prussians did allow the French to hold elections and set up a new government. France once again became a republic. But the new government was weak and divided. A majority of the delegates elected to the new National Assembly in 1871 were conservatives, hostile to democracy and eager to restore the rule of kings.

In the years following the war, Bartholdi created three sculptures designed to maintain French patriotism at fever pitch. Each expresses the emotional qualities of Romanticism which were then fashionable in sculpture, and which the sculptor later incorporated into the Statue of Liberty.

The first was called "The Curse of Alsace." It reflected the rage and grief shared by all Frenchmen over the Prussians' annexation of the province of Alsace, which was Bartholdi's birthplace. This sculpture of bronze and marble features the despairing figure of a woman. She is kneeling beside the body of a dead French soldier and grasping the flag which has fallen from his lifeless fingers.

Bartholdi's second war monument was dedicated to the French soldiers killed in battle. It lies in a cemetery in Colmar, and at first glance almost seems to be one of the gravesites. But the stone lid covering the grave appears to have been split open by a bronze hand reaching out from the grave, struggling to grasp a sword which lies nearby. This was Bartholdi's way of expressing the French people's unquenchable determination to take up the fight against the Germans one day and to wreak vengeance for the horrors inflicted on their country.

Better known than either of these is his great "Lion of Belfort." It honors the French border city which was besieged by the Prussian invaders for 103 days, suffered 73 days of bombardment with half a million shells, but never surrendered. Bartholdi carved it in the living granite of the hillside just below the Belfort fortress. His gigantic lion, about seventy-three feet long and over thirty-six feet high, is shown rearing up and roaring defiance. A smaller replica can be seen in Paris, at Place Denfert-Rochereau on the Left Bank.

All of these works were still in the future as the war came to an end in 1871, and Bartholdi was again invited to dinner at Laboulaye's home. Bartholdi reminded his friends of the upcoming centennial of American independence. It was just five years away. Hadn't the time come, he asked, to revive professor Laboulaye's "passing thought" of a monument whose cost would be shared by the peoples of both countries? What more fitting memorial could there be to their mutual struggle in the American Revolution? And wouldn't a nationwide campaign on behalf of such a memorial help to promote republican sentiments among the French?

The monument, Bartholdi thought, should somehow express a single powerful concept: liberty. But at that point he was still not entirely certain as to its final form.

He volunteered to journey to America, at his own ex-

Bartholdi's extraordinary monument to the French dead of the Franco-Prussian War.

The sculptor's defiant "Lion of Belfort."

would sound out the Americans, explain the
an to them, and try to persuade them to share
ost.

Laboulaye, despite a lifetime's study of the American political system, had never visited the United States. He urged Bartholdi to go. He must get to know the people, explore the country from coast to coast, and bring back his impressions. And if Bartholdi could come up with the right image for the statue, Laboulaye told him, "a plan that will excite public enthusiasm, we are convinced that it will . . . produce a far-reaching moral effect." Laboulaye and his associates would launch a fund-raising campaign in France to finance it.

Bartholdi began to plan the momentous voyage at once. Knowing that Laboulaye corresponded regularly with many prominent Americans, he asked for letters of introduction to opinion makers in the press, the government, the arts, literature, and the universities.

"Trying to glorify the republic and liberty over there," he wrote to Laboulaye, "I shall await the day when they may be found here with us." The sculptor shared Laboulaye's scorn for the monarchists who then dominated the French government.

Bartholdi arrived in New York in June 1871. He was thrilled by the harbor's magnificent setting and bustling commerce. As his ship sailed through the Narrows into the Upper Bay, he noticed an island situated not far from its center. Every person arriving at that great gateway to America had to sail right past the island on the way into port.

He knew at once that he had found the ideal site for his monument. As he wrote later, "The statue was born for this place which inspired its conception."

The site was then called Bedloe's Island. Bartholdi

was delighted to discover that, as he wrote to Laboulaye, "It belongs to the government; it is land *common to all the states.*" Surely the government could be convinced to turn over at least part of the island for the French people's planned gift.

Inspired by the spectacular location, Bartholdi could now begin to visualize the Statue approximately as it would appear on the site. He made a watercolor sketch, which has survived to the present. It portrays Lady Liberty almost, but not quite, as we know her today. In the sketch her left hand holds a broken vase, an ancient symbol of slavery. He soon substituted a tablet, cradled in her left arm, bearing the historic date July 4, 1776. Later, Bartholdi also shifted her position somewhat, and the pedestal was completely redesigned.

Bartholdi began a round of visits to the many distinguished Americans for whom Laboulaye and his friends had given him letters of introduction. In New York he met two influential editors, Horace Greeley of the *New York Tribune* and George W. Curtis of *Harper's Weekly.* In Massachusetts he had a delightful visit with the celebrated poet Henry Wadsworth Longfellow, who pronounced the Liberty project "a grand plan" and promised to help.

Bartholdi chatted with President Grant at the latter's New Jersey summer home. The sculptor wrote his mother that he had found the president "a cold man . . . but quite affable." He had shown Grant his project. "He likes it very much, thinks that securing the site would not be a very difficult problem, [and] that the project [should] be submitted to Congress."

Moving on to Washington, Bartholdi was shown around on the Fourth of July by the famous orator, Senator Charles Sumner of Massachusetts. On various other

The original concept of the Statue, sketched during Bartholdi's first visit to the U. S. in 1871.

stops he met the philanthropist Peter Cooper, the financier Cyrus Field of Atlantic Cable fame, the scientist Louis Agassiz, the influential Philadelphia newspaper publisher Colonel Joseph Forney. "I seek in each town," he wrote to Laboulaye, "individuals willing to take part in our enterprise. Up to now I have found some everywhere."

Bartholdi was probably being overoptimistic. It is true that the Americans he spoke to all reacted cordially to the Liberty project. It was after all very flattering to

Americans, especially those descended from the heroes of the Revolution and those recently involved in the Civil War. And he was careful to emphasize that the French would pay the cost of the Statue.

But there is no record that these men took any action on behalf of the project after his departure. Bartholdi had not, in fact, requested any specific action as yet. He had only planted the seeds of his cherished idea; they would bear fruit before very long.

Particularly significant for Bartholdi's personal life was the renewal of his friendship with the American artist John LaFarge, whom he had known in Paris. LaFarge opened his home and studio in Newport, Rhode Island, to Bartholdi. Over the next decade, the sculptor did much of his creative work on the Statue there.

Bartholdi's journey took him to Chicago, Pittsburgh, St. Louis, Denver, Salt Lake City, Sacramento, San Francisco. He was impressed by the savagery and immensity of the American landscape, and made sketches and paintings everywhere. "Everything is big here," he informed Laboulaye in amazement, "even the green peas." The Americans' love of bigness, he may have been thinking, might help sway them to support his colossal project.

Equally impressive to him were the "admirable patriotism . . . the strong sense of duty and concern for education" which he found among the people. But certain American attitudes impressed him less favorably. He wrote to his mother that of all the many difficulties still blocking his project,

> the greatest, I think, is in the American character, which is not very open to things of the imagination. The important thing is to find a few people who have a little enthusiasm for something other than themselves and the Almighty Dollar.

In the fall of 1871, after five months in America, Bartholdi returned to France. As soon as he could, he met with Laboulaye and his other old friends. He described his experiences in detail, emphasizing the Americans' positive response to his proposal. His friends were, naturally, delighted.

They were even more gratified when he told them of the theme he had decided on for the statue: "Liberty Enlightening the World." It seemed a perfect statement of their hopes for the spread of freedom everywhere, and especially for its final triumph in France.

Finally, he showed them his sketch of the Statue on its island site. Laboulaye and the others could see at once how right his choice of location was.

Thus encouraged, Bartholdi cast aside all modesty. He was determined, he said, to create nothing less than "a statue of colossal proportions which would surpass all that have ever existed since the most ancient times." Critics and historians have been debating ever since as to whether Bartholdi actually achieved that exalted goal.

At one point, Bartholdi was questioned about a supposed resemblance between the Statue and his unfulfilled Suez project. Bartholdi was infuriated by the insinuation that he had merely transplanted his Egyptian *fellah* to America. Their only common feature, he replied forcefully, was

> that both hold a light aloft. Now . . . how is a sculptor to make a statue which is to serve the purpose of a lighthouse without making it hold that light in the air? Would they have me make the figure . . . hiding the light under its petticoat?

In the political sphere, the project still faced serious obstacles. The struggle in France between the monarchists and the republicans remained undecided. A campaign on behalf of a monument which some Frenchmen would undoubtedly view as propaganda for a revolutionary idea might do more harm than good. Bartholdi and his friends decided to wait.

A chance arose very soon to test public opinion on both sides of the Atlantic. The people of Paris had passed through a terrible time in the winter of 1870–71. Their city was then besieged by the Prussians, and dire shortages of food caused actual starvation. As soon as the siege was lifted, the people of New York had sent generous aid.

As a token of appreciation, the French government decided in 1873 to present a larger-than-life bronze statue of the Marquis de Lafayette to the city of New York. The man who had been George Washington's close friend and aide during the Revolution, and who had obtained substantial French assistance for the Americans throughout the great struggle, was the ideal symbol of the traditional friendship between the two peoples.

President Adolphe Thiers chose Bartholdi to execute the statue. The sculptor went to work immediately, and was able to exhibit a plaster model that same year. It depicted Lafayette at the age of twenty, upon his first arrival in America in 1777. The young French aristocrat is shown stepping onto American soil, holding his sword with the hilt pressed to his heart, symbolically offering his life in the cause of the Revolution. The statue received unanimous praise.

The finished work in bronze was delivered to the Americans in time for the celebration of the centennial of the Revolution in 1876. It was erected in Union Square, in downtown New York City, where it still stands. The Americans were pleased and grateful. Bartholdi and his friends felt that the success of the Lafayette gift was a good omen for the much grander expression of French-American amity and prodemocratic sentiment which they were planning.

2
THE LADY TAKES SHAPE

To the sculptor, form is everything and nothing—
nothing without the spirit, everything with the idea.
—Victor Hugo, in a note to Bartholdi after
seeing the Statue of Liberty in Paris, 1885

Bartholdi had thought deeply about the Statue even before he began to experiment with actual models and sketches. He started out with three extremely general notions. He knew that it would be very large, perhaps the largest statue ever built. He knew that the design must express his chosen theme of "Liberty Enlightening the World." And finally he knew the monument must be clearly recognizable as a tribute to the American struggle for freedom.

But what specific form would it take?

Once, at an earlier stage of his career, Bartholdi had sketched out an image of America as a proud, vigorous young man. The man's arms rested on a machine, symbolizing America's growing mastery of technology. A horn of plenty at the man's side illustrated the abundance flowing from America's farms. At his feet lay the shattered idols of the past. Certainly these attributes expressed the power, the material wealth, the forward-looking spirit, which had so impressed Bartholdi during his first visit to America in 1871. But he felt these were not right for his embodiment of liberty.

He might have considered the most ancient of all models, the goddess of liberty worshiped by the Romans. They built a temple to her in the third century B.C. But she symbolized merely the personal status of being free as opposed to being a slave.

Then there was the monument erected by order of King Louis Philippe, who mounted the throne of France after the revolution of 1830. It was a "Genius of Liberty" atop a tall column in the Place de la Bastille. The "Genius of Liberty" was a male figure carrying a flaming torch in one hand and a broken chain in the other.

Another model Bartholdi undoubtedly considered was one of the most celebrated paintings of his time. Entitled "Liberty Leading the People," it had been painted by the great French Romanticist Eugène Delacroix as his homage to the revolution of 1830. It portrayed a heroic young woman, her clothes half torn away, a flag raised in her right hand, a musket in her left, leading her fellow revolutionaries forward over the bodies of their fallen comrades. Emperor Napoleon III had felt this painting was such a dangerous incitement to rebellion that for many years he ordered it hidden from public view.

Bartholdi admired Delacroix's masterwork, but rejected it as a basis for his own project. Its violence was out of keeping with the lofty idea he wished to express.

Still another possibility was the traditional symbol

Columbia. Her figure appeared on many American coins in those days. She wore a robe of the ancient style, and looked very much like a traditional Roman deity. Her name was of course derived from that of Christopher Columbus. There were many who felt that Columbia would have been a more suitable name for the lands of the New World than America, which was taken from a much lesser-known explorer, Amerigo Vespucci.

But Columbia was a rather aloof and complacent figure. She was almost always shown calmly seated rather than actively involved in human affairs. Bartholdi had no intention of using such an unexciting image. He did however decide to clothe Liberty in a robe of antiquity like that worn by Columbia.

Bartholdi finally determined to create his own adaptation of a type of statue that was fairly common in his day. Several well-known nineteenth-century monuments featured a majestic female figure holding up some sort of symbolic device. Some held a banner or sword; others held a cross, a wreath of victory, or even a torch. He would start with that general concept, but would endow it with attributes specifically tailored to his unique subject.

Bartholdi experimented with a variety of forms. First he reviewed some of his preliminary sketches for the proposed Suez lighthouse. The earliest of these, modeled in clay in 1867, had depicted the Egyptian female *fellah* raising the torch in her right hand. In subsequent sketches he tried out the effect in her left as well. For the Statue of Liberty he decided that the right hand was somehow more appropriate.

As for the Lady's left hand, he thought at first that it should hold some traditional symbol of the victory of freedom over bondage. He tried the ancient device of a broken vase, then changed it to something more readily understood: broken chains.

Ultimately he had a better idea. The object to be held in the left hand should establish the Statue's American identity. After considering several possibilities, he came up with an appropriate solution. The left hand and arm would hold a tablet commemorating the date of the adoption of the Declaration of Independence, July 4, 1776. As was customary with sculptured dates in Bartholdi's time, it would be carved in Roman numerals: JULY IV MDCCLXXVI.

But the Statue still needed some element dramatizing the triumph of liberty. Bartholdi resolved to show the Lady striding vigorously forward, treading upon the broken shackles of slavery.

In his Suez sketches, the figure had worn an unadorned crown. The Lady too would wear a crown, he decided, but it would be embellished with seven rays. This sign of a radiant crown had a long history. Ever since ancient times it had denoted the sun's radiance to the seven known planets. In more recent Christian statues it had symbolized the inspirational power of religious faith. Bartholdi intended the seven rays of his Statue to signify the influence of liberty radiating out over the seven seas and the seven continents.

There was another factor that influenced his choice of the radiant-crown device. The Bartholdi family emblem was a sunburst.

The crown was originally intended to serve a second purpose as well. In the words of a brochure sent out by the Statue's sponsors in 1875, "at night a luminous aureole projected from the head (through windows in

left

1869 model of the proposed lighthouse for the Suez Canal, with the torch in the left hand. The sculptor had not yet conceived the idea of rays emanating from the crown.

right

An early model of the Statue of Liberty. Bartholdi later reworked the awkward position of the left hip.

the crown) will radiate on the farflowing waves of the ocean. . . ." From the very first the monument had been conceived as having a dual function, as idealistic symbol and as practical lighthouse.

The hoped-for radiant effect was illustrated in a slightly revised version of Bartholdi's 1871 watercolor sketch of the Statue on its Bedloe's Island site. The new sketch incorporated the sculptor's latest ideas into the 1875 brochure.

But whose face would the Statue present to the world? Bartholdi had no problem with this choice. His adored, highly patriotic, sometimes domineering mother was a direct descendant of a famous Alsatian hero of the French Revolution. It was she who had first taught him the great French Revolution ideals of Liberty, Equality, and Fraternity. Bartholdi still consulted this imperious woman about every major decision. He could think of no more imposing model. The resolute face of Charlotte Beysser Bartholdi became the face of Liberty.

By the end of 1870, the sculptor had worked out most of the basic questions relating to the Statue's form. He then turned to its complex technical problems. Of what material should he make it? What technique should he use to support and stabilize its gigantic form? How would he equip it to stand against centuries of fierce winds and storms in New York harbor?

He considered first some examples of outsized statues built in the past. There were the Colossus of Rhodes and the immense carvings he had admired in Egypt. There was Phidias's thirty-seven-foot gold and ivory statue of the goddess Athena, which the Athenians of ancient times had worshiped in the great temple, the Parthenon.

More recent, and more interesting to Bartholdi be-

Bartholdi with his mother, "the face of Liberty."

cause of the method used in its construction, was the seventeenth-century statue of Saint Charles Borromeo. It stood on the shores of Lake Maggiore in northern Italy, with its seventy-six-foot form towering above a forty-foot pedestal. Bartholdi had seen it while returning from one of his trips through Egypt. The statue had been built by the *repoussé* method, and Bartholdi decided that this technique would best suit his new project.

In the *repoussé* method, the "skin" of the statue is made of thin sheets of copper or some other light but durable material. Skilled craftsmen carefully beat these sheets into the desired shapes with specially designed mallets. The copper sheets are then placed in their proper locations and attached to a framework, or armature, in such a way that none of them weighs directly upon any of the others. Instead, they are supported by the framework from inside the statue.

Repoussé statues are essentially hollow shells. They tend to be much lighter than statues produced by other methods. Yet they are stable enough to resist even the stormiest weather. Their skin is firmly yet flexibly supported by the interior framework—which in turn can be solidly anchored in the pedestal. The skin can also expand or contract easily and naturally in response to the wind as well as to temperature changes.

Bartholdi had several choices for the material of the skin. He preferred copper because it was light and strong and easily worked. It would also be resistant to the salt-laden air of New York harbor. Exposed to the air for long periods, copper develops a rich green covering known as a patina, which would be both protective and attractive.

The *repoussé* technique has been known since ancient times. It had reached a high degree of perfection by the nineteenth century. Bartholdi wrote that the copper skin of the statue of Saint Charles Borromeo was "only a millimetre in thickness, and yet the whole work has stood until today, that is to say, for two centuries."

Bartholdi and his engineers made detailed calculations of gravity, wind resistance, and other physical factors that would affect the Statue. They determined that a thickness of about three thirty-seconds of an inch would meet all the requirements for the skin. That is only about as thick as two pennies placed face to face. The skin's actual thickness would vary slightly from one point to another as the material was hammered into shape.

Bartholdi was also determined to outdo a colossal monument that the Germans had been working on since the 1840s, but which they did not complete until 1875. This was a statue of Arminius, a German warrior of ancient days who had led his countrymen against the Romans. It too had been built on the *repoussé* system. It stood as tall as the Saint Charles Borromeo but on a pedestal more than twice as high. The Arminius appears even more imposing because the triumphant warrior brandishes a mighty sword above his head.

Bartholdi made the bold decision to build his Statue to an unprecedented height of 151 feet from the base to the torch. It would tower almost exactly twice as high as the Saint Charles Borromeo or the Arminius. The exact height of the base and pedestal would be determined later, but they too would surpass all existing models.

His calculations showed that a figure that tall would have a waist thirty-five feet thick. Its face would be ten feet wide. The nose would be almost four feet long; each eye, two and a half feet wide. Each index finger would be eight feet long. The longest ray in the crown would rise eleven and one-half feet. What such a colossus would weigh, Bartholdi could only estimate. (At its completion the Statue weighed about four hundred fifty thousand pounds, including the interior framework. In modern terms, the Statue's weight is about twice the load lifted by the *Saturn 5* rocket which sent three astronauts to the moon in 1969.)

Having made most of the basic decisions, Bartholdi wasted no more time. He hired a skilled staff and arranged for the biggest workshop in Paris to be reserved exclusively for the Statue. It was located not far from the Place de l'Étoile, the great Paris circle that is topped by the Arch of Triumph and from which twelve avenues radiate, including the famous Champs-Élysées.

All that remains today of this site where the Statue was built is a plaque attached to one of the buildings that have replaced the workshop. The plaque was placed there only recently, at the insistence of an American who felt that so historic a place should not be forgotten.

Bartholdi's next step was to engage a renowned architect, Eugène Emmanuel Viollet-le-Duc, to design the structure that would support the Statue from within. Viollet-le-Duc came up with a clever but cumbersome idea. The supporting element would be formed of compartments filled with sand. The compartments would be designed so that each could easily be emptied, without affecting any of the others, whenever repairs to any section of the skin became necessary.

Viollet-le-Duc died in 1879, before he could carry his ideas into practice. Bartholdi replaced him with an engineer who was rapidly acquiring a reputation as the most brilliant innovator of his generation. His name was Alexandre Gustave Eiffel. He was famous for designing several of Europe's most spectacular bridges. He had pioneered a method for supporting them with extremely light but immensely strong and flexible iron towers, called pylons. Eiffel would later create the tallest iron pylon of them all, the world-famous tower that bears his name and that virtually symbolizes the city of Paris.

Eiffel shared Bartholdi's appreciation for the unique power of the colossal in sculpture. He realized that such works might be disparaged by certain critics, but he defied them:

Alexandre Gustave Eiffel, brilliant designer of the Statue's interior framework and, later, of the Paris tower that bears his name.

> There is in the colossal an attraction, a particular charm, to which the theories of ordinary art are hardly applicable. Does one suppose it is by their *esthetic* value that the Pyramids have struck man's imagination so strongly?

Eiffel had no problem with the basic concept for the Statue's interior framework, or armature. Its main component would be an iron pylon like those he had created for his bridges. But how would the pylon be linked to the Statue? The connections must give maximum support, yet remain flexible enough to adjust swiftly and smoothly to heat, cold, and wind. The problem demanded creative solutions. Eiffel devoted the next four years to this quest.

There was one extra complication, stemming from Bartholdi's original design. The raised arm and torch swung out from the line of the Statue's body at a perilous angle. Eiffel persuaded the sculptor to alter his design a little, so that the arm would rise at an angle closer to the vertical of the Statue. But it would still need a second supporting armature, which would have to be designed with special care.

Eiffel addressed himself first to the linkage between the main armature and the skin. He conceived a system of light iron trusswork (similar to a web) that would reach out from his pylon to many points on the skin. An intricate network of slender strips of iron called strapwork would line the inside of the skin. Little iron "saddles," riveted to the skin, would hold the strapwork tightly in place. The ends of the light iron bars forming the trusswork would be bolted to the saddles, effectively linking skin and armature.

Thousands of copper fasteners, or rivets, had to be driven through the skin and strapwork to hold them together, but Eiffel made sure they would be invisible from the outside. Surprisingly few of Eiffel's rivets have needed replacement in the century since they were carefully countersunk through the skin.

Eiffel was well versed in physical science. He knew that if the iron of the strapwork and the copper of the skin were allowed to come into direct contact, they would interact harmfully through an electrical process known as galvanic action. He insulated them from each other with a layer of asbestos impregnated with shellac.

The Statue itself was of course grounded against light-

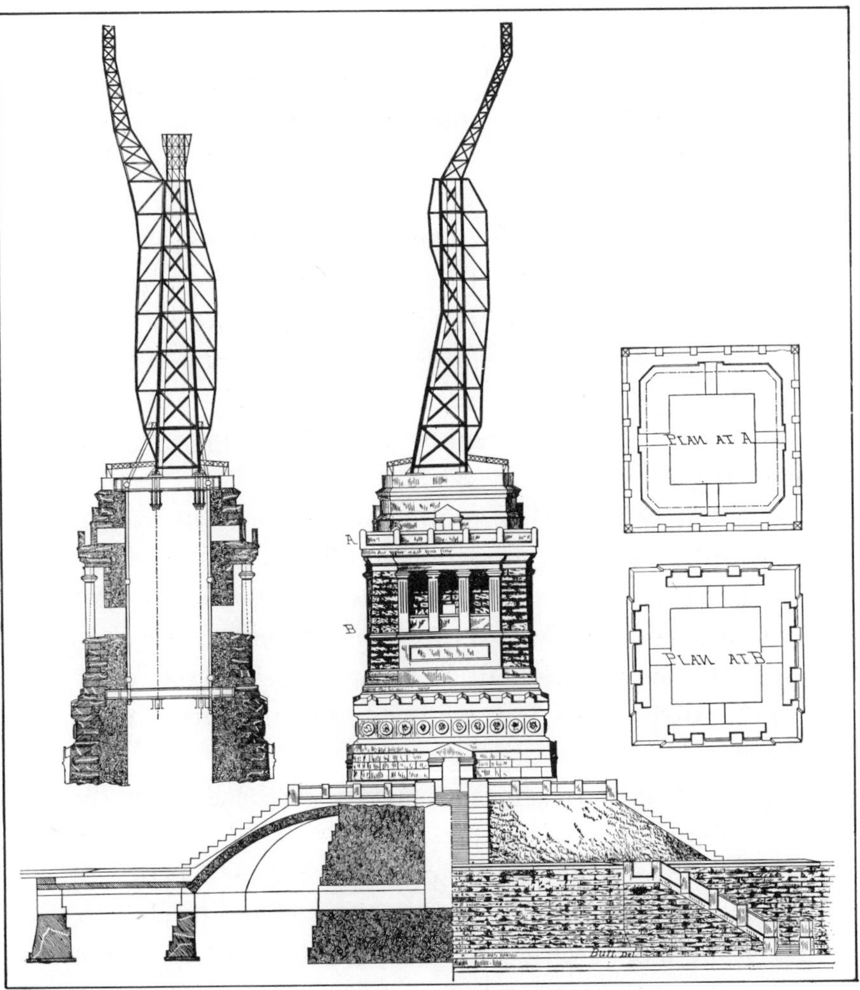

Eiffel's durable yet flexible iron framework, showing how it is anchored to the pedestal.

ning. It has never suffered any damage from that source.

To deal with the extra problem of a supporting framework for the arm and torch, Eiffel had to devise an original solution. He designed a sixty-five-foot girder, which reaches upwards at a steep angle but is firmly anchored in the upper two levels of the pylon.

In the days when visitors were still permitted to climb up to the torch and out onto its little observation balcony, they could feel this secondary armature sway as it responded to the wind. On gusty days this could be a scary experience. In 1916 the arm was closed off to the public.

However, the arm's alarming tendency to sway was not the only reason for the closing. The cramped space inside the arm allowed for only one narrow steel ladder. Thousands visited the Statue every day. Many of these people would have loved to climb up to the little balcony around the torch and enjoy the spectacular open-air view from there.

The balcony could accommodate only twelve persons at a time. Only one at a time could climb up or down on the ladder. The resulting jams were becoming horrendous. The arm had to be closed not only because of its frightening movement, but also to prevent the build-up of crowds in such a narrow and constricted part of the Statue.

The linkage between the girder inside the arm and the central pylon was rebuilt and reinforced as part of the major renovation that preceded the celebration of the Statue's centennial in 1986. The arm and torch were safer and more stable after that, but it remained doubtful that the torch would be reopened to the public.

The overall result of Eiffel's brilliant planning was an astonishingly strong yet supple structure. Throughout the Statue, the flexible iron bars of the trusswork acted as springs. They gave the skin secure support; yet they allowed for all the elasticity required by the buffeting of wind and weather.

Eiffel's design foreshadowed two notable developments in twentieth-century engineering and architecture. First, the aerodynamic principles underlying his design were soon to be applied in the new industry of aircraft manufacture. Airplane components, especially the wings, were built according to the methods he had proven in the Statue.

Second, his solution to the Statue's internal support problem made it one of the first examples of what is now known as "curtain-wall" construction. This concept revolutionized the construction of modern skyscrapers. In the earliest tall buildings, the exterior walls had to support their weight. Hence the outer walls had to be massive, giving them a not very pleasing look.

Many high-rise buildings put up since the Statue of Liberty have followed Eiffel's example. Their exterior "curtain walls" are built of attractive light substances such as glass, aluminum, or copper. The structural elements supporting the buildings' weight are concealed inside. Exterior elements on the upper floors do not weigh upon those below them; their weight is carried by the interior framework.

Working with a young architect named L. A. Boileau, Eiffel had actually designed and constructed one of the first such buildings as early as 1876. It was the Bon Marché department store in Paris. It had glass walls on all three facades, with circular pavilions at the corners. The store still stands, but a masonry skin was added in the 1920s.

Inside the Statue, Eiffel provided the means for visitors to view the interior as they climbed to the observation chamber in the crown. He designed a double spiral stairway that wound around the center of his pylon. Visitors would walk up one stairway and down the other. Each consisted of 171 steps, the equivalent of a twelve-story climb. Eiffel thoughtfully included little resting stations at regular intervals along the way.

Eiffel's original stairways were rather narrow. They

were widened and improved as another feature of the renovation of the mid-1980s.

With the designs for both interior and exterior virtually complete, actual construction began in 1875. Bartholdi personally supervised work on the Statue as it proceeded inside a huge shed. He proved to be a hard-driving taskmaster, overseeing every detail and insisting on flawless work.

The sculptor also demonstrated remarkable executive ability. He administered the labor of hundreds of workmen on dozens of simultaneous tasks. He saw to the purchase and delivery of all the required materials. He tinkered endlessly with the design, perfecting it at every stage of production. He carried on a ceaseless campaign to publicize his project and raise funds for it.

At the same time, Eiffel's pylon started to rise on the grounds of the workyard, just outside the shed. The two men had to coordinate their work closely, making certain that the two components—armature and skin—would fit exactly when they were finally brought together.

Bartholdi began with a series of extremely precise, enlarged copies of his original four-foot clay model. The first of these plaster enlargements was one-sixteenth the final size. It was quadrupled to a one-fourth-size model, which served as the basis for the full-scale Statue. At each stage, the sculptor carefully smoothed out or eliminated all unnecessary lines or wrinkles. He was an emphatic believer in the rule that a colossal statue must not contain any detail that might distract from the overall effect.

The next phase started with a division of the one-fourth copy into 210 segments. Each of these was then reproduced at full size by the extremely complex "point-

The Lady's left hand, in an early stage of construction. Bartholdi is the bearded figure at lower right.

ing-up" method. Once a full-size plaster section was complete, carpenters cut slender boards and fitted them tightly to the contours of the plaster in a precise pattern called a latticemold. The resulting forms looked somewhat like honeycombs. They would protect the plaster as the coppersmiths went to work with their mallets.

The coppersmiths' work too required several steps. When they were through, the Statue's shiny new skin in 300 separate copper sheets was ready for mounting.

Bartholdi made no effort to build the Lady from the ground up. She was constructed in many separate and often unrelated sections. The arm and torch were the

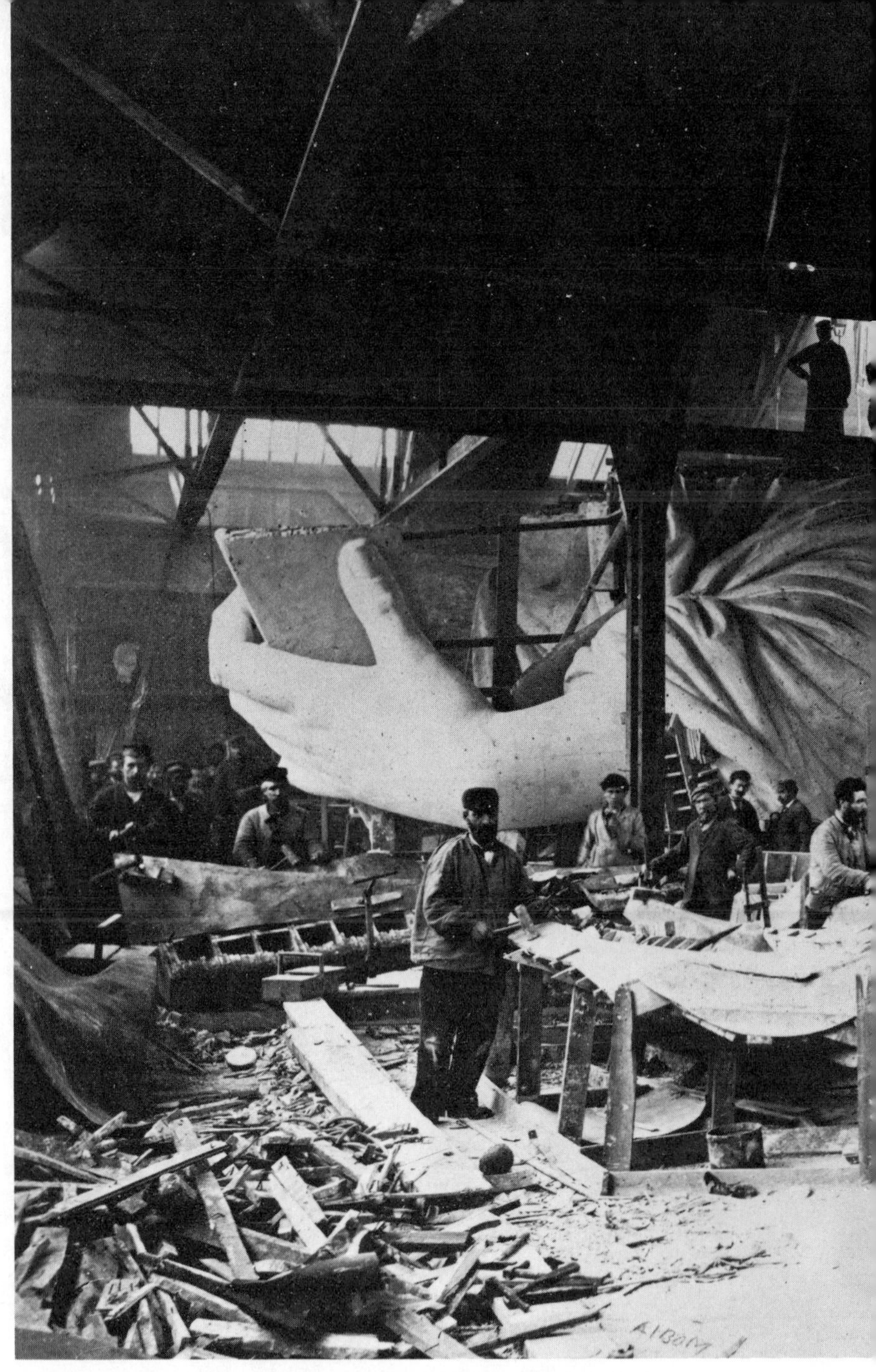

At left, the completed plaster model of the left hand. In the background at right, the 1/4-size model from which it was copied.

first parts to be finished. The head was next. This system was often confusing to visitors.

On one occasion, a group of journalists visited the workshop. The French newspaper *Le Gaulois* reported that one of them pointed at what looked like a big siege gun and asked what it was.

"*Mais, monsieur,*" came the reply, "that's the torch. Look at this one-sixteenth scale model. There's your siege gun. See how it tapers? Viewed as high as it will be placed, and lighted from above, this torch that you can walk down in will seem to have quite ordinary proportions."

"And this round bulk—what is that?"

"The elbow, sir. The elbow and part of the forearm."

"And those five huge rifles?"

"They're the fingers. Over there, you see the hand. It's finished."

A correspondent for the *New York World* reported seeing "fifty workmen hammering for their lives on sheets of copper." They looked like Lilliputians, he wrote, against the huge bulk of the Statue's parts. They reached the Statue's back hair "by means of ladders running from stage to stage of a high scaffolding." He described his own sensations: "I mounted the scaffolding with them and stood on a level with her awful eye—some thirty inches from corner to corner—to be engulfed in her gaze."

He observed a six-foot-tall workman working on Liberty's face; the man's frame reached from the line of her lips only to the middle of her brow. "Her lips, from dimple to dimple, were as long as my walking stick. . . ."

By July 1882 the Statue's body had been built up to its waist. Bartholdi, who was beginning to show a real talent for publicity, invited the reporters to luncheon.

When they got to the workyard he led them inside the base of the Statue. Climbing a ladder as far up as the Statue's knee, they were astonished to find a platform on which tables had been set for a fine meal. Everything they needed was hauled up with a rope and pulley.

The newsmen enjoyed themselves enormously. Still amazed by the experience, the reporter for *Le Temps* informed his readers that "twenty men can comfortably lunch in the knee of this statue."

The building of the Statue was to some extent a nationwide effort. Some of the parts were built elsewhere and then transported to the Paris workshop. One of the fingers, for example, was made by a coppersmith living as far away as Montauban, a town in the south of France. But wherever they worked, the craftsmen had to follow Bartholdi's instructions down to the last detail.

Inevitably, there were those who had doubts about the Statue's design. One misguided example was an 1884 article in the *London Daily News*. It noted that some experts "think the Statue will never stand, and that the winds and the waves will play havoc with it. It is not solid enough, and never can be." So much for the experts.

Two years later the *New York Times* published a critical report that looked at first as if it might have serious implications. It was a statement supposedly made by Major David P. Heap, chief engineer of the U.S. Lighthouse Department, which then had charge of the Statue. The major was quoted as declaring that the Statue was "structurally weak, defenseless against Time's erosive tooth, and liable to become a burden and a sorrow" to the government.

Heap was particularly concerned about the sometimes frightening effect of strong winds on the upraised

The interior framework and the secondary girder for the upraised right arm rise out of the half-completed skin. At left, visitors try out the torch balcony.

right arm. He suggested that it might be prudent to remove the ladder leading up to the torch.

The *Times* defended the Statue against the charge that it had no defense against erosion. "Articles in copper . . . have come down to us from the dim ages preceding the Fourth Olympiad." The Statue's own chief engineer, General Charles P. Stone, sent a letter to the newspaper making a similar argument. The general added that the ascent through the arm to the torch might be "uncomfortable," but he insisted it was not dangerous.

The controversy ended when Major Heap replied to General Stone. In a tone of considerable embarrassment, Heap claimed he had merely told a reporter that he had "found some vibration in the arm, as was to be expected." He still felt visitors should not be allowed up there, "as their extra weight would necessarily increase the vibrations and in time might weaken the supports. . . ." But Heap then went on to say that "all this talk about corrosion, or about the arm dropping off, was simply rot." He had absolute "confidence in the stability of the Statue."

Heap's confidence has been amply justified. The Lady's skin has required remarkably few repairs, considering how exposed her island is to the harshness of the elements. As for her stability, it has remained unshakable. Only Heap's suggestion about closing off the arm has had to be adopted.

◦ 3 ◦

THE LADY TRIUMPHS IN FRANCE

Compared to our statue, the Colossus of Rhodes is but a clock ornament.

— Edouard de Laboulaye, 1875

Designing the Statue was only one of the problems Bartholdi faced. Before it could actually be built, France had to undergo profound political changes. And even when that painful process was accomplished, the Statue's sponsors still had to find ways to finance it.

The prospects for Bartholdi's project had appeared very dubious in the early 1870s. It looked as if the monarchists were about to triumph over the believers in democracy. A new French monarchy would almost certainly forbid the erection of a monument honoring liberty—especially when that liberty had been won through violent revolution. America was still the only major republic in a world dominated by empires, kingdoms, and princely states.

After considerable squabbling, the monarchists agreed on their candidate to become the new king. Their choice was the Count of Chambord. He was a descendant of the Bourbon dynasty, which ruled France until the French Revolution. The count was so sure of himself that he even began to sign his correspondence as "Henri V of France."

Then the monarchists' plan hit a totally unexpected stumbling block. Ever since the Revolution the nation's flag had been the tricolor, consisting of three broad vertical stripes of red, white, and blue. The people felt that this was their flag, and they cherished it. But the arrogant Count of Chambord absolutely refused to rule under the tricolor. He regarded it as a symbol of revolution, liberty, democracy, and everything he detested. He insisted on restoring the old Bourbon flag, a white banner adorned with three fleur-de-lis designs.

The count's supporters pleaded with him in vain to change his mind. They explained to him that there was no way the old royal flag could be restored without causing a tremendous political upheaval. The count remained stubbornly unmoved. The frustrated monarchists had no choice but to give up all their long-held hopes and dreams. On the petty issue of the flag, the whole idea of reestablishing a monarchy in France collapsed.

By 1875, Laboulaye and his fellow liberals had won control of the French Parliament. A new constitution had been drafted, but it still didn't mention the word "republic" (the term "republic" denotes any form of government that is not headed by a hereditary ruler, such as a king). It was at that point that Laboulaye had what historians regard as his finest hour.

He rose on the floor of the Chamber of Deputies and summoned up all his well-known powers of eloquence to plead for the republic. At his final words, "For the love of our beloved country, have pity, pity on France!" the entire audience broke into tears and cheers.

Laboulaye then proposed an amendment to the constitution, which would define France finally and forever as a republic. Narrowly defeated at first, his proposal triumphed two days later. In the weeks that followed, Laboulaye played a key role in designing a new, democratic constitution for France. It remained the nation's governing document for over half a century.

One rather curious provision of the new constitution was at first intended to placate the monarchists and conservatives. One-third of the members of the new Senate were to be "irremovable"; once elected, they would remain in office for life. The monarchists and conservatives were expected to win most of these seats. To everyone's surprise, most of them were won by the liberals. Laboulaye was among those elected as one of the new life-tenure senators.

With the final victory of the forces of democracy in France, the Statue's sponsors felt that they could at last proceed to the realization of their dream. In August 1875 Bartholdi completed his first fully detailed plaster model. It stood two and a half feet high.

In that same month Laboulaye and his friends organized the formal body that would see the project through to completion: the Union Franco-Américaine (French-American Union). Its first action was to issue a statement to the press, announcing the great plan and calling for financial contributions from the public.

The Statue itself, the statement explained, would be funded by the French. The Americans would be expected to finance the pedestal.

"Let each bring his mite," the press release concluded, "the smallest subscriptions will be well received. Let the number of signatures express the sentiments of France."

As originally conceived, the Statue was to be considerably smaller than it eventually became. Its cost was at first estimated at about 240,000 francs ($60,000; the franc was then valued at about twenty-five cents in American money). This was a very considerable sum in those days. The equivalent in today's inflated currency would probably amount to at least fifty times as much. But this preliminary estimate turned out to be much too low.

The liberal French press was generally enthusiastic, but the monarchist and conservative newspapers were still smarting over their recent political defeat by Laboulaye and his supporters. They heaped scorn on the whole undertaking. Leading the opposition was *Le Figaro,* which published a long article sneering at the notion that the Americans really felt any gratitude or affection at all for France.

The project's sponsors ignored such carping. Laboulaye was already thinking ahead to the problem of obtaining American aid. He wrote to the editor of the *Courrier des États-Unis,* the publication which served the French colony in America. Laboulaye expressed optimism about the French people's response to the project. "Would it not be possible," he asked, "to organize in New York a committee corresponding to ours?"

The French living in New York promptly formed the committee Laboulaye had suggested. They launched fund-raising activities at once. But Laboulaye knew better than to expect the relatively small number of Frenchmen in the United States to provide the large funds that would be needed.

Fortunately, an influential and interested American was in Paris at that time. This was Colonel Joseph W. Forney, a Philadelphia newspaper publisher and important Republican politician. Bartholdi had met him in America, and had won him over to the project. Forney promised to help, pledging that if New York did not eventually take the Statue, he would see to it that Philadelphia did.

Forney was among the two hundred French and American guests invited to attend a formal dinner, held at the Hôtel du Louvre in Paris on November 6, 1875, at which the French-American Union's fund-raising campaign was officially inaugurated. Dominating the affair was a huge, colored "transparency," showing the Statue as it would eventually appear on its New York island. Forney and the new American ambassador, Elihu Washburne, were among the speakers; but as usual it was the silver-tongued Laboulaye who most deeply stirred the audience.

"Compared to our Statue," he declared, "the Colossus of Rhodes is but a clock ornament." He went on to contrast Liberty with an enormous monument recently erected by the Germans in honor of their military victories. It had been fabricated from captured weapons.

"The statue which we would cast," Laboulaye pointed out, "is not made of cannon taken on the field of battle. Each of its limbs has not cost a thousand men's lives, and has not caused countries, widows, and orphans to shed tears. . . ."

A most welcome notice was passed around during the dinner on behalf of England's largest manufacturer of gas lamps. Recognizing that one of the Statue's main purposes was to serve as a lighthouse, he pledged that as soon as the Statue was completed, he would "furnish, free of all expense, the necessary light with my burners . . . to establish this as the first and best light in the world." (This generous offer soon proved unnecessary. Thomas A. Edison perfected the electric light in 1879, allowing ample time for its use in the Statue.)

This first fund-raiser by the French-American Union was a great success. It raised some 40,000 francs.

Other contributions now began to flow into the Union's coffers. The city of Paris gave 2,000 francs. The seaport of Le Havre contributed 1,000 francs. Rouen gave 500. Some 181 French cities and towns eventually gave varying amounts. As a matter of principle the national government was not asked to contribute, and it did not.

One of the most appropriate contributions came from the firm of Japy Frères, prominent copper merchants. They announced their intention to give all the copper needed for the Statue's exterior. Their generous gift was valued at about 64,000 francs.

The French-American Union then sent out fourteen thousand subscription blanks. By the end of that first year, pledges had been received from all over France, totaling nearly 200,000 francs.

The contributors made up a decidedly mixed group. There were, first and foremost, thousands of schoolchildren and ordinary citizens who genuinely believed in the ideals that the Statue would express. There were descendants of Frenchmen who had fought in the American Revolution, notably the Lafayette and Rochambeau families. There were the Freemasons, traditional supporters of liberal causes; their Grand Master, Henri Martin, was a close friend of Laboulaye and an officer of the French-American Union. There were all those who had fought beside Laboulaye in the recent struggle for the French republic, and who viewed the campaign for the Statue as a means of promoting democratic ideas in France. There were businessmen who had commercial ties with the United States. There were investors in the proposed Panama Canal, who hoped to gain the support of American public opinion.

But from the rich and powerful, from the aristocracy, from the conservatives, there came only contempt and resentment. To them, the Statue represented propaganda for rebellion, mob rule, and bloodshed.

After the public's first gratifying response, contributions to the Liberty fund slackened. Meanwhile, the moneys already received were quickly exhausted as work on the Statue got under way.

The project's sponsors cast about for new ways to stimulate public support. They decided on a gala musical fete, to be held at the Paris Opera on April 26, 1876. The famous composer Charles Gounod created a cantata (composition for orchestra and chorus) specially for the occasion, taking its title from the Statue: "Liberty Enlightening the World." Gounod personally conducted the performance. The chorus, according to a report in the *New York Times,* consisted of "800 picked singers from the various Orpheus societies."

Gounod's work was the first of several attempts to capture the spirit of the Statue in verse. Its opening stanzas reflected a formal, high-flown style that was already old-fashioned:

> I Liberty, old in years, in this hour
> Am triumphant, but in more than a name.
> The world has made, wishing beauty and power,
> My body bronze and my spirit of flame. . . .

I cast out into the dark night's haze
When forth my beacon flares are sent,
To the ship in distress my light's rays,
And to the wronged, enlightenment.

Despite such well-intentioned efforts, the affair was unsuccessful. The Opera's regular subscribers, who were almost all of the wealthy classes, shunned it. It attracted few others. A bare four hundred persons attended, including a few American tourists who might have read about the Statue in their hometown newspapers. Only 8,000 francs was collected.

The first component of the Statue to be completed was the right forearm upholding the torch. It was shipped off to Philadelphia, where it quickly became one of the most popular exhibits at the great Centennial Exposition of 1876. Visitors who climbed the ladder inside the forearm and emerged onto the little balcony encircling the torch enjoyed a fine view of the fair.

When the Philadelphia exposition came to an end, the forearm and torch were removed to New York City. There they were exhibited for seven years in Madison Square Park, again arousing considerable public excitement and incidentally helping to bring in donations. Finally they were shipped back to the Paris workshop for inclusion in the Statue.

Within two years the head was finished as well. It was placed on exhibition at the Paris Universal Exposition, to which it had been carried on a cart drawn by twelve horses. Bartholdi later wrote that "about 40 persons were accommodated" in the observation room inside the head, which stood about seventeen feet high.

But funds were again running low. The French-American Union decided to try a lottery. The required government approval was quickly obtained. Business

The Statue's head on display at the Paris Universal Exposition of 1878.

firms all over France were persuaded to donate over five hundred valuable prizes. A total of three hundred thousand tickets were to be sold both in France and in America, at the extremely reasonable price of one franc each (about twenty-five cents in American money).

The hope was that the lottery would take in all the funds still needed to complete the Statue. It came very close but did not quite cover the estimated final cost, which by now had risen to nearly one million francs.

Another scheme that proved successful was the idea

of producing four hundred terra-cotta copies of Bartholdi's four-foot clay model of the Lady. These exceptionally detailed copies, probably the most accurate reproductions of Liberty ever made, were then sold for three thousand francs each in France, and three hundred dollars in the United States. A special feature of this promotion was that the buyer's name could be engraved into the clay before the models were placed in the furnace for baking. These models are worth considerably more today, but they are hard to find.

Bartholdi also arranged for a French firm, Avoiron et Cie., to produce equally attractive imitation-bronze casts (actually copper-plated zinc). Only six of these were produced in the four-foot size; these eventually became extremely valuable because of their rarity. More copies were cast of a smaller model, about two feet tall.

Using these and other promotional devices, the Union ultimately accumulated the required sum. On July 7, 1880, a formal "Notification Dinner" was held at a Paris hotel, and the Americans were duly notified that there was no further obstacle to completion of the Statue.

Soon afterward, Laboulaye wrote to an old friend in New York, Mary L. Booth. Of French descent, she had translated Laboulaye's writings in the past. He happily informed her of the successful fulfillment of the French-American Union's fund-raising goals. With luck, the monument would be ready in time for the hundredth anniversary of the signing of the peace treaty that ended the American Revolution in 1783. (Laboulaye turned out to have underestimated the time needed for the Statue's completion by about a year. An additional two years would be required for financing and building the pedestal in the United States.)

Laboulaye reminded Mary Booth of how much grander the new Statue would be than the celebrated Colossus of Rhodes. That ancient monument, he noted, had lasted nine hundred years. He expressed the hope "that the statue raised as a souvenir of the friendship of France and America will last well until 2900."

Laboulaye added the wish that he would be able to come to America for the Statue's unveiling, but his health was already failing, and he doubted he would live that long. Sadly, Laboulaye lived neither to visit the America he admired so greatly nor to witness the triumphant unveiling of the Statue whose idea he had conceived. He died in 1883 at the age of seventy-one. Thousands of freedom-loving French men and women mourned at his funeral. The *New York Times* saluted his passing, noting that he had been "a firm friend of the Union . . . and in many ways endeared himself to Americans."

Bartholdi outlined the status of work on the Statue in an 1883 letter to William M. Evarts, chairman of the American committee recently formed to raise funds for the pedestal. The Lady, said the sculptor, was already rearing her head above the houses surrounding the workshop.

Bartholdi sent Evarts a fascinating series of photographs taken inside the workshop, showing fragments of the Statue in various stages of completion. Bartholdi authorized the American either to show them to the committee or to publish them. He promised to send more photos of the Statue as it was mounted on Eiffel's framework outside the workshop.

Work now moved forward without interruption, reaching completion in June 1884. The event was celebrated in Paris with a banquet given by American ambassador Levi P. Morton in honor of the French-

American Union. Interest in the project in the United States had reached such a peak by this time that the description of the banquet appeared on the front page of the *New York Times.*

The *Times* reported that the prime minister of France, Jules Ferry, had attended the banquet. The principal speaker was Ferdinand de Lesseps, the brilliant promoter who was chiefly responsible for the building of the Suez Canal. De Lesseps had now replaced the deceased Laboulaye as head of the French-American Union.

Shortly afterward, Ambassador Morton sent a telegram to his superior, the secretary of state. The French prime minister, Morton wrote, would soon join with the French-American Union "in the formal transfer of the Statue of Liberty to me as representative of the President." The French government was even planning to provide a naval vessel to transport the monument to America. Morton requested formal instructions.

The secretary promptly replied with authorization for Morton to accept the Statue on behalf of President Arthur, with all due thanks to the French government and the French-American Union.

Appropriately, the ceremony took place on the Fourth of July, 1884. De Lesseps delivered the presentation address, concluding with a hope shared by all involved. "We now transfer this great statue" to the American people, said de Lesseps, "and trust that it may forever stand as the pledge of friendship between France and the great republic of the United States."

In the meantime, a certain amount of feeling had been building up among some French citizens that they would be sorry indeed to lose the magnificent statue now looming over the Paris rooftops. Some three hundred thousand of them had actually visited the workshop and marveled at the work in progress. It was, after all, a creation of French genius, paid for by French men, women, and children. And it expressed an idea that was at least as French as it was American.

Americans living in Paris quickly became aware of this spreading sentiment. They decided to do something about it. On September 1, 1884, they issued a statement to the newspapers, calling for support from their fellow Americans for a new project: the creation of a replica of the Statue, one-fourth as large, or about thirty-eight feet tall, to be presented to the city of Paris.

As things turned out, the replica did not have to be an entirely new creation. Instead, the funds collected were invested in a copy of one of Bartholdi's own carefully crafted plaster models. The full-scale Statue had in fact been reproduced with extreme precision from this one-quarter-size model, using the special "pointing-up" method perfected by Bartholdi.

The donations came in so quickly, and the replica was built with such ease, that the American colony in Paris was able to present it in the spring of 1885. It was originally placed at what seemed the most appropriate location, the Place des États-Unis (United States Square). Ambassador Morton made the presentation, and the head of the municipal council accepted for the city of Paris.

Four years later, at Bartholdi's suggestion, the model was moved to a much prettier site on an island in the Seine, the Île des Cygnes (Island of Swans). Now the model, like its big sister, stood at last in a maritime setting. Bartholdi felt strongly that Liberty should not be surrounded by buildings, but should raise her torch in an open environment of sun, wind, and waves.

Another ceremony was held at the new site. This one was attended by the president of France, who did the unveiling. The replica can still be seen there today, not far from the Eiffel Tower. A plaque on the pedestal expresses the feelings of its American donors:

> We revere the France of the past because her soldiers have enabled us to become a nation, and we love the France of today because she has joined us in the cause of free government.

On New Year's Day, 1885, Bartholdi pronounced the full-sized Statue ready for shipment to America. Dismantling began, with the separate parts carefully packed into 214 huge crates. Some of these weighed as little as 150 pounds, while others tipped the scales at three tons.

Each crate—and each part inside—was painstakingly numbered and identified. The crates were loaded onto the French warship *Isère* in reverse order, so that the first pieces to go up on the site in New York harbor would be the first unloaded.

The *Isère* sailed from Rouen on May 21, 1885. Now it was up to the Americans.

· 4 ·
THE LADY SEEKS FRIENDS IN AMERICA

Every man, woman and child in our country should feel an interest and own a share, however small, in this grand gift of the French to our people. . . .
— Jessie Truelove of Brooklyn,
in a letter to the *New York Times,* 1877

Bartholdi had done his best to stir up interest in the Statue during his 1871 visit to America. He did win assurances of support from a select group of prominent individuals. But most Americans remained unaware of the project. It was the formation of the French-American Union in Paris in 1875 that first attracted serious attention in the American newspapers.

The newspapers' attitudes varied. William Cullen Bryant's *New York Evening Post* reported on the new plan with enthusiasm. The *New York World* gave the Statue an admiring two-column spread. The *World* compared it favorably with the Colossus of Rhodes and other giant monuments of the past.

Laboulaye won the favor of the *Tribune* with an explanation of the project's aims that could not fail to please Americans. The people of France, he wrote to the *Tribune*'s editor, wished to join with the Americans in their celebration of "that noble Liberty which represents the glory of the United States, and which enlightens the modern people by its example."

Only the *New York Times* seemed hostile to the whole idea. The *Times* sarcastically suggested that the Statue should be erected at the Battery, a small park on the southern tip of Manhattan, rather than all the way out on Bedloe's Island. "The thousands of persons who would be anxious to write their names in pencil on its legs," scoffed the *Times,* "would dislike the trouble of being compelled to hire a small boat to reach it."

But if any single event can be said to have marked the Statue's debut in America, it was New York's mammoth celebration of the nation's hundredth birthday on July 4, 1876. There was a huge torchlight parade through the city that evening. The marchers' destination was Madison Square. Every building there had been colorfully decorated and brilliantly lit up. The New York Club was particularly dazzling, its Fifth Avenue front ablaze with red, white, and blue Chinese lanterns.

Over the entrance there hung a tremendous full-color transparency showing the Statue as it would eventually appear, its copper-colored form gleaming in the sunlight on the island in the windswept bay. It seemed only fitting that the goddess of liberty should preside over the Independence Day festivities.

Bartholdi was in New York that day. He had come as part of the official French delegation to the Philadelphia Centennial Exposition. He spent the Fourth of July at the location he had chosen for the Statue out on Bedloe's Island, working with a group that included several army engineers. Bartholdi made detailed sketches of the site, seeking to determine exactly how the Statue should be placed for the best effect. The engineers carried out a preliminary survey, explored the existing structures on the island, and studied the composition of the soil.

The island had a strange and varied history. It was originally called Oyster Island, back in the days when the Dutch ruled the colony. Apparently its only use at that time was as a place for gathering oysters and hunting rabbits.

In 1670, after the British took over, the island was for some reason declared a "privileged place, where no Warrant of attachment or arrest shall be . . . served unless it be by ye Governor's special warrant." Why it should have been designated a haven for persons in trouble with the law remains unclear. But it did not remain a haven long. Some years later a man named Hicks, who happened to be the last man ever executed in the United States as a pirate, was hanged there.

A Dutch immigrant named Isaac Bedloe eventually acquired ownership of the island from the British. New York City bought it from the Bedloe family in 1750 for 1,000 English pounds (about $5,000). Its isolated location made it suitable for use as a "pesthouse"; that is, a place for quarantining people suspected of haboring contagious diseases.

Fifty years later the United States faced the threat of a new war with Great Britain. Keenly aware of Britain's overwhelming naval power, New Yorkers were concerned about the defense of their harbor. New York decided to turn the island over to the U.S. government, which would begin the process of fortifying it.

The U.S. Army set up an emplacement for coastal guns on the island between 1808 and 1811. War broke out in 1812. The installation on Bedloe's Island was hastily expanded into a full-scale fortress. It took the shape of an eleven-pointed star. Each of the eleven "points" was designed as a defensive bastion, with each holding a gun platform. The fortification was later named Fort Wood in honor of a colonel who was killed in action during the war. Despite all these preparations the island never saw any military or naval action, then or later.

During the Civil War, Fort Wood served as a recruiting station for Union troops. By the mid-1870s, just as the Statue's sponsors were attempting to secure a portion of the island for their project, the army was already preparing to abandon it. Ultimately, the Statue was erected almost exactly above the fort's central point. Its thick walls in their starlike eleven-point configuration still stand today, as staunch as ever, seemingly ready to defend the Statue against the ravages of wind and tide.

In 1876 the sponsors' immediate problem was to publicize the Statue and convince the American people that it deserved their support. Their task was eased considerably in mid-August, when the forearm and torch arrived in Philadelphia for the Centennial Exposition. Carefully removed from its twenty-one giant packing cases, assembled and set up on the grounds of the exposition, the exhibit's popularity helped stimulate widespread interest. On a single day, officially designated New York Day, some one hundred twenty-five thousand persons visited it. Stories and articles began to appear in newspapers and magazines throughout the country.

The gratifying publicity rose to a new peak in September. The occasion was the formal presentation of Bartholdi's statue of Lafayette to the city of New York. The French consul general made the presentation, with the mayor responding. Then the French national anthem, the "Marseillaise," was sung, followed by "Hail, Columbia" ("The Star-Spangled Banner" was not chosen as America's national anthem until 1931).

At that point a signal was given, and Bartholdi himself pulled the rope unveiling his statue. The crowd burst into applause, and the air was instantly split by salutes from several cannon that had been brought to Union Square for the occasion. Then the guns on Governors Island and those in the Brooklyn Navy Yard thundered a reply, echoed by salvoes from two naval vessels at anchor in the port, U.S.S. *Plymouth* and U.S.S. *Minnesota.* Finally, three cheers rang out for the proud and delighted sculptor, who acknowledged them with a bow and a broad smile and a genial wave of the hand.

Bartholdi was later commissioned to create another heroic bronze monument, which showed Lafayette with one hand clasped in a firm handshake with Washington while the other gripped the flags of France and America. This one now adorns Morningside Park, in upper Manhattan.

September 1876 was also the month in which the first American committee was organized to promote the Statue. Its chairman was John Jay, grandson of the first chief justice of the U.S. Supreme Court. Another committee was shortly set up in Philadelphia. Neither group proved particularly effective at raising funds. The project seemed to be going nowhere.

Bartholdi realized that he would have to take personal responsibility for winning the American people to his side. In the months that followed, he demonstrated considerable skill as a promoter. One of his most effective ideas was to arrange for production of a handsome, gilded, but relatively inexpensive Statute of Liberty medal, which he awarded to any and all Americans who performed services on the Statue's behalf. He also sought out and obtained invitations to speak to clubs and associations of every kind—an excellent way to keep his name, and the Statue, in the papers.

The sculptor was also alert to the commercial possibilities. Sooner or later there would be a public demand for miniature copies of the Statue and all sorts of other souvenirs. Bartholdi saw that he must act to protect his proprietary rights. He took detailed drawings of the Statue to the U.S. Patent Office in Washington, and copyrighted his creation. From that point on, anyone attempting to profit from the sale of copies or other objects related to the Statue would legally be obligated to pay royalties to him.

Bartholdi's foresight should have made him a rich man in the course of time. The sad fact is that it did not. He received some relatively small sums from the sale of miniatures of the Statue produced under committee sponsorship, but few royalties on other copies and souvenirs. Because of a faulty contract with an American company, he never received a penny from its highly profitable sale of Statue models. The best he could do was to obtain a court order, in December 1885, halting these unlicensed sales. But other companies were already on the market with still more imitations. The creator of the Statue of Liberty died a poor man.

Most of the publicity produced as a result of Bartholdi's efforts was favorable. But the *New York Times* remained skeptical. Its highly respected and influential editor, George Jones, suspected that there might be some sort of fraud scheme behind the project. A few days after the forearm and torch were put on exhibition in Philadelphia, he wrote a scathing editorial casting doubt on the sculptor's motives as well as his competence. Jones supposed it was "only natural" that New Yorkers would be flattered by the gift of "several hundred feet of bronze female." But there must be some sort of skullduggery in the sculptor's odd method:

> The construction of a woman by making a solitary arm was not the way any really able and earnest sculptor would go to work. Had the French sculptor honestly intended to complete the Statue of "Liberty," he would have begun at the foundation, modeling first the boot, then the stocking, then the full leg. . . .

Jones went on to trace the constantly rising estimates of the Statue's cost. Work on it in the Paris workshop, he noted, had had to be suspended at that moment until additional funds could be collected. The French were doubtless expecting the Americans to pay the remaining expenses, which might amount to as much as 2 million francs. This was an exaggeration, but Jones apparently felt it was necessary to make his final point:

> No true patriot can countenance any such expenditure for bronze females in the present state of finances, and hence, unless the French change their minds and pay for the Statue themselves, we shall have to do without it.

Bartholdi was understandably annoyed by Jones's insinuations. He quickly came up with an effective technique for changing the editor's mind. He went to work on some of his friends in Philadelphia.

The results became apparent within a few days, at a banquet given in Bartholdi's honor by the French exhibitors at the Philadelphia Centennial Exposition. All through the dinner, the guests could admire Liberty's forearm and torch on their lakeside pedestal, gleaming under brilliant lights sparklingly reflected in the water. Colonel Joseph Forney, the Philadelphia newspaper publisher, delivered the after-dinner address. He announced that if New York were to decide against accepting the Statue, "the city of Philadelphia would leap at the opportunity to get possession of it." Forney proposed the immediate formation of a Philadelphia committee for this purpose.

Though Bartholdi had done all he could to get the Philadelphians to offer this new proposal, he revealed his true feelings about it in a letter to Laboulaye. "If we wished to place the Statue in Philadelphia," he wrote, "we would find all the money needed." But with his eyes and his hopes still firmly fixed on his chosen site in New York harbor, he quickly added that a Philadelphia location "would not be the same thing." He had, however, given the Philadelphians "the idea of buying the arm." He could make a copy of it easily enough—an improved and refined copy, at that.

As it turned out, no sale of the arm and torch was ever completed. After the exposition closed they were returned to Paris and incorporated into the Statue.

Within three days, Bartholdi could enjoy the effect of his strategy. In a witty new editorial in the *Times,* George Jones completely reversed himself. He accused the Philadelphians of planning an act of "piracy." He poured scorn on their supposed efforts to "make their respectable inland town a great seaport." It was laughable for Philadelphia to try to "seize upon a New York lighthouse [the Statue] and set it up in the Delaware River, where it could guide the midnight eelfisher and the belated muskrat to their respective homes."

Blithely ignoring the accusations he had made against the French only a few days earlier, Jones now expressed confidence that they would contribute their "full share" for the funding of the Statue. He concluded with a serious warning to New Yorkers that they must get busy and raise the additional funds that were still needed, "unless we are willing to lose the lighthouse."

The New Yorkers' response came in January 1877. At a meeting at the elite Century Club, a new American Committee for the Statue of Liberty was set up to replace the unsuccessful earlier one. Its chairman was an experienced and influential politician named William M. Evarts. Most of its other members too were practical men of affairs who could be expected to drive hard for results.

If the members needed any added motivation, they received it in the form of a huge new oil portrait of the Statue. The work was by Edward Moran, an artist much admired for his seascapes. Entitled "Liberty Lighting the World's Commerce" (sometimes called "The Commerce of Nations Paying Homage to Liberty"), it showed Liberty in her original copper hues, shining in the sun as fleets of ships under full sail and flying the flags of many nations paid tribute to her in a colorful procession around Bedloe's Island.

At the dinner that featured Moran's painting, newly appointed chairman Evarts announced the first official estimate of the pedestal's cost. It would amount to $125,000. (This turned out to be a very considerable underestimate.)

The first public response came within days of the an-

Edward Moran's imaginative portrait, "Liberty Lighting the World's Commerce" (1877), painted when the Statue was still years from completion.

nouncement. It took the form of a letter to the editor of the *Times,* signed by one Jessie Truelove of Brooklyn. "Not only the rich," she wrote,

> but every man, woman and child in our country should feel an interest and own a share, however small, in this grand gift of the French to our people. . . . Allow me the pleasure of heading [the list of contributors] with the enclosed gold dollar, trusting that increase will be added to it a hundred thousand fold.

Welcome as it was, Miss Truelove's example produced no great flood of imitators. The committee faced years of arduous campaigning before the needed funds could be raised.

Meanwhile, Evarts got to work. His first move was to obtain assurances of support from the federal government. He drafted a congressional resolution which for the first time acknowledged that the government had a responsibility "to provide for the care and preservation of this grand monument of art." The resolution authorized the president to accept the Statue, and "to set apart for the erection thereof a suitable site upon either Governor's or Bedloe's Island, in the harbor of New York. . . ."

The problem of choosing between these two sites was quickly resolved. General William T. Sherman, Civil War hero and now chief of staff of the U.S. Army (which controlled both locations), bowed to Bartholdi's expressed preference and designated Bedloe's Island as the Statue's future home. The dream that Bartholdi had cherished since 1871 had moved a big step closer to fulfillment. A part of the island, which he had been so pleased to learn was "common to all the states," was at last assured as the site for his Statue.

The resolution went on to require the president, as soon as the Statue was completed, to "cause the same to be inaugurated with such ceremonies as will serve to testify the gratitude of our people for this expressive and felicitous memorial of the sympathy of our sister republic. . . ."

With the draft of the resolution in his hand, Evarts personally took it to the White House and persuaded President Grant to sign it. Then he had an influential Democrat introduce it in the House of Representatives, while an equally important Republican did the same in the Senate. The resolution was passed without a single dissenting vote. Its easy acceptance was undoubtedly due at least in part to the sponsors' constantly repeated assurances that the monument would cost the government nothing. The French were paying for the Statue, and the American committee had pledged to raise all costs for the pedestal from private sources.

At the same time, the committee published an appeal for funds. Even the *New York Times* published the full text of this document. But editor George Jones's attitude had by no means swung fully over to the Statue's side quite yet.

Jones vented another blast of sarcasm in February 1877, when the forearm and torch were moved to New York after the closing of the Philadelphia exposition. The exhibit, thirty feet high, was set up in Madison Square, where it was to remain for seven years. New Yorkers enjoyed it as much as the Philadelphians had. Paying 50 cents for the privilege, they clambered up the steel ladder inside the arm and were rewarded with a fine view of the surrounding area from the little balcony round the torch. But Jones had other ideas. He contended that this was only the first step: "Other pieces

The forearm and torch on display in Madison Square, New York City, 1877–1884.

. . . will be erected in the parks and squares of the city."

Jones then went on to involve the Statue in one of the stormiest political conflicts of the day. The presidential election of 1876 had resulted in a stalemate. The nation went through months of suspense. It was the spring of 1877 before a special commission finally decided in favor of the Republican candidate, Rutherford B. Hayes.

His Democratic opponent, Governor Samuel J. Tilden of New York, had actually won a majority in the popular vote. Jones was outraged; as he saw it, New York's own candidate had been unjustly defrauded of his well-earned victory. Jones now proposed, only half in jest, that when the Statue's legs arrived they should "be placed upside down in the middle of the Central Park lake. . . . The spectator could then fancy that Liberty had 'drowned herself' " after learning that the election of the president of the United States had been "stolen."

The elevation of Hayes to the presidency proved beneficial to the Statue committee in at least one respect. The new president named Evarts as his secretary of state. The committee could now bask in reflected glory and prestige, for Evarts remained its chairman.

But nothing seemed to help. The ensuing months proved unfruitful for the committee's fund-raising efforts. Repeated appeals to the public produced little. In October 1877 the committee's frustration found indignant expression in a letter to the editor of the *Times* by one William Minturn, a citizen of Hastings-on-Hudson.

Minturn argued that the Americans themselves should have "raised a monument to this [French-American] alliance which was our birth," instead of waiting for the French to do it. All that was asked of us now was to finance the pedestal. "A short time ago," he related,

> an Englishman took me shamefully to task for our treatment of Lafayette's memory and the French. I had not a word to say in our defense. . . . For God's sake, let us bare our backs and do the work with our own hands, rather than let Englishmen and Europeans say we have tumbled so low we do not even know how to receive a gift.

The American public remained unresponsive. Donations to the pedestal fund barely dribbled in. The committee's embarrassment became especially painful in July 1880. That was when the French-American Union held its "Notification Dinner" in Paris, and notified the American committee that all funds required for building the Statue were in hand, so that work could go forward without further delay. The French were doing their part; the Americans seemed to be up against a blank wall.

The humiliated American committee couldn't bring itself to reply to the French notification for six months. Evarts finally wrote to Laboulaye in December. He expressed himself in flattering and optimistic terms that were more of a tribute to his experience in diplomacy than his realism:

> We have not the slightest doubt that our compatriots will gladly furnish the money for the pedestal, and that we shall be able to complete its construction in ample time for it to receive the noble statue which your genius and your generosity have offered us. . . .

The facts dismally refused to support Evarts's optimism. By November 1882, when the committee held another formal fund-raising dinner, collections were still lagging.

· 5 ·

THE LADY IN DISTRESS

As the rich citizens of New York have shown such apathy in this matter, let the poorer citizens move. The World *. . . offers to receive all sums of $1.00 and upwards that may be sent to its care. . . .*

—Joseph Pulitzer, in an editorial in his *New York World,* 1883

Despite its money woes, the committee decided to move ahead with planning for the pedestal. It appointed one of the foremost American architects of the day, Richard Morris Hunt. He had been the first American ever admitted to the Ecole des Beaux Arts in Paris, then the most respected of all schools of art and architecture. He subsequently designed much-admired mansions for some of America's wealthiest families. Hunt and Bartholdi may have met during the sculptor's visit to America in 1876.

One of Hunt's first acts after receiving the commission was to write to Bartholdi. He requested the fullest possible technical information about the Statue, as well as suggestions concerning the pedestal. Bartholdi replied at once, sending detailed drawings and calculations prepared by his engineers.

Hunt promptly worked out a detailed plan for the pedestal, and submitted it to the committee. He expected construction work to require about nine months. (Because of the delays caused by the committee's constant financial problems, the pedestal was not actually finished for nearly four years.) Hunt's plan made one additional fact uncomfortably clear: The eventual cost would mount a good deal higher than Evarts's original estimate of $125,000. The committee nevertheless approved the plan.

Also hired at about this time to take charge of construction as engineer in chief was General Charles P. Stone. A graduate of West Point and veteran of both the Mexican and Civil wars, Stone had met Bartholdi in Egypt in 1869. The general was then on leave from the U.S. Army to command the army of Egypt for Ismail Pasha. He had supervised a wide range of construction projects.

Bartholdi was in Paris in the early 1880s, overseeing the completion of the Statue. He was increasingly distressed about the Americans' money troubles. On October 31, 1882, he wrote of his concern to Richard Butler, secretary of the American committee, who had become a close personal friend. Bartholdi described the mounting scorn of the French press for the apparent failure of the fund-raising effort in the United States. Bartholdi urged the American committee to send some sort of public statement designed "to end the ridiculing of the press." The French were about to apply to their government for official transportation of the Statue to the U.S., "but as you will understand we must first be assured of the feelings of the Americans. . . ."

The American committee could offer no helpful reply.

Perhaps, thought Bartholdi, some additional publicity would help. His earlier ploy, prodding the New Yorkers by pretending that Philadelphia was about to grab the Statue, had drawn considerable newspaper attention. He decided to try the same trick with Boston. To his gratification, the leading citizens of that city responded just as eagerly as the Philadelphians had.

Once again, it was the *New York Times* that took up the cudgels against the out-of-towners' rash intrusion. In this "latest stab," fumed editor George Jones, Boston

> has stretched forth her hand to grasp that pleasing symbol of Franco-American amity. . . . This statue is dear to us, though we have never looked upon it, and no third-rate town is going to step in and take it from us. Philadelphia tried that in 1876, and failed. Let Boston be warned in time that she can't have our Liberty.

The people of New York would prefer to see the monument "smashed into minute fragments before it shall be stuck up in Boston Harbor." But, just as he had done before, Jones found it necessary to warn New Yorkers that the problem stemmed from their own miserly reluctance to fund the Statue. The American committee must now "bestir itself" and "rebuke [Boston's] impudence."

Toward the end of November, the committee sponsored a "monster mass meeting" at the Academy of Music. A model of the Statue occupied center stage; it was backed by Edward Moran's imposing painting of the Lady receiving the homage of the nations.

Evarts was one of the main speakers. For the first time, the audience heard from him the sobering news that the pedestal was now expected to cost $250,000—twice as much as his own original estimate. Evarts eased the bitter pill by promising that one-sixth—perhaps as much as one-fifth—would come from the members of the committee. The members, all quite well-to-do, did in fact contribute handsomely.

One example was Joseph W. Drexel, chairman of the executive committee, who saw to it that his firm, the investment banking house of Drexel, Morgan & Co., gave $5,000. This was one of the largest contributions the fund ever received.

The committee then published a pamphlet for nationwide distribution: *An Appeal to the People of the United States in Behalf of the Great Statue of Liberty Enlightening the World.* It asked communities all over the country to form subcommittees to promote the Statue's cause. A few cities and towns did so, but many were surprisingly hostile. The fund drive continued to limp along.

In a further attempt to reach out beyond the borders of New York, the committee hired a man named Mahlon Chance, well known for his persuasive powers, and sent him on a fund-raising tour of the western U.S.

The committee had collected about $75,000 up to that time. This was certainly an impressive sum for that era. But it amounted only to a bare beginning on what was needed. And at least ninety percent had come from New Yorkers, reflecting one of the project's most stubborn problems.

There was a widespread feeling elsewhere in the United States that the Statue was intended solely as a gift to New York, rather than as a tribute to the nation as a whole. Besides, New York was notorious as the nation's richest city, with the highest proportion of millionaires. Why should the rest of the country contribute to a monument that would only beautify the harbor of selfish, affluent New York?

Responding to the committee's difficulties, the *Times* now swung the full weight of its prestige and influence behind the fund drive. It published an editorial explaining why the response so far had been so disappointing. The newspaper argued that the rest of the nation did indeed have a moral obligation to contribute.

"The idea of such a present and such an honor from one nation to another was startling," the editorial admitted. "When you are told to your face that you are a model, you immediately begin to doubt your right to the honor." But Americans should now be getting used to the idea and should accept it.

Another question was understandably troubling many Americans, the editorial continued: Was the gift addressed to New York City, or New York State, or the United States? There could be no real doubt on this score; the Statue of Liberty was clearly and undeniably "a monument to the Union." The proper response would therefore be "a popular subscription from every part of the country."

From that date forward, the *Times* consistently gave the fund drive helpful coverage. In mid-January 1883, for example, it published a list of major contributors. These included the wealthy merchant John Jacob Astor ($2,500), the philanthropist Peter Cooper ($1,000), and the firm headed by the U.S. ambassador to France, Levi P. Morton ($1,000). Subsequent lists duly publicized the not overly impressive generosity of such notables as steel magnate Andrew Carnegie ($500).

Publication of these lists was doubtless intended as a nudge to other wealthy individuals. It didn't work. New

York's numerous millionaires proved immovably indifferent if not actively hostile to the Statue. They seemed to share the attitudes previously exhibited by the French artistocracy, viewing the monument as an unwelcome symbol of revolution and disorder.

Another list that kept getting longer was that of New York's rivals for possession of the Statue. Philadelphia's and Boston's claims had already been answered. Now it was the directors of the Washington Monument Association, reported as making "indirect overtures" to have the Statute erected on the monument grounds, in the nation's capital.

The monument's sponsors apparently felt that Washington was a more appropriate setting for the Statue than New York. They probably considered the site they were offering doubly suitable, since it would place the Statue dedicated to the struggle for independence close by the towering new obelisk dedicated to George Washington.

Bartholdi, though he was not consulted, would almost certainly have disagreed. No offer from any other city—and there were to be several more such offers—ever altered his feeling about the incomparable spectacle of the Bedloe's Island setting. In any case, the Statue committee ignored the Washington "overtures."

Then, to the pleased surprise of the Statue's frustrated sponsors, a dynamic new personality joined their cause. His name was Joseph Pulitzer, and over the next two years he was to become nothing less than the savior of the pedestal fund drive.

Pulitzer had immigrated to the United States from Hungary at the age of seventeen. German-speaking, he served in the last months of the Civil War with a Union cavalry regiment comprised chiefly of German immigrants. After the war he discovered that there was a substantial German population in St. Louis, Missouri, and he settled there.

His first newspaper job was as a reporter on a German-language daily, the *Westliche Post.* It was the start of one of the most remarkable careers in the history of American journalism.

By 1871 Pulitzer had become part owner of the newspaper. He soon moved on to ownership of his first English-language paper, the *St. Louis Dispatch.* It was virtually bankrupt when he bought it. Then the owner of the equally troubled *St. Louis Post* offered to merge the two papers. Pulitzer accepted at once. Endlessly energetic and creative, he swiftly turned the new *Post-Dispatch* into a profitable and respected newspaper. It still ranks among the nation's most esteemed publications.

In May 1883 the now well-to-do Pulitzer was passing through New York. His health had always been frail, and he was on his way to Europe in search of the finest available medical treatment. He abandoned these plans when he unexpectedly learned that the *New York World* was for sale. That daily belonged to Jay Gould, a notorious financial manipulator. It had long been losing money. Gould used it only to promote his money-making schemes and cared nothing for its journalistic reputation.

Gould wanted $500,000 for the *World.* Pulitzer got him down to $346,000, and made the purchase. His uncanny editorial skills almost instantly transformed the formerly lackluster paper into a rapidly growing popular success. Pulitzer made the *World* a reform-minded spokesman for the city's laboring classes and an outspoken, uncompromising critic of the rich and powerful.

He was determined to win acceptance for it as "the people's newspaper."

At the same time, he felt no embarrassment about using every technique he could think of to catch and hold the public's attention. He was one of the first to use large-type banner headlines (in those days most newspaper headlines were only one column wide and rarely as much as a half-inch high); he ran all sorts of sensational feature stories and promotional stunts; he used pictures and cartoons on a scale never seen before; he frequently gave front-page coverage to the most spectacular crimes of the day; and above all, he fearlessly and consistently attacked corruption wherever he and his reporters could find it.

Pulitzer found a story that was a likely crowd pleaser during his very first days on the *World*. It was the fund drive for the Statue of Liberty. This cause appealed to him for several reasons. First and foremost, he sincerely believed in the ideals embodied in the Statue. Second, he saw at once that the main reason for the fund drive's halting progress was the resistance of the city's wealthier classes—whom he regarded as a prime target. Third, he was convinced that ordinary citizens could be persuaded to care about the Statue and contribute to it, if only they were approached in a way that appealed to their natural humanity and patriotism. And finally, he saw splendid opportunities for building the *World*'s circulation through a crusade on behalf of the Statue.

Pulitzer opened fire with an editorial blast on May 14, 1883. He raked New York's millionaires for spending fortunes on their own pleasures while refusing the relatively small sums needed for the pedestal. The whole disgraceful episode could have been avoided, he asserted, with "the dash of one millionaire's pen."

He announced that the *World* would conduct its own fund drive. It would accept contributions in any amount. Pulitzer even added a likeness of the Statue to the *World*'s masthead.

This first campaign by Pulitzer had great potential, but it turned out a failure. Probably he was too involved in reorganizing his only recently acquired *World*, reshaping its whole style and outlook, and building its circulation. The *World* itself was still suffering from the unsavory repute it had acquired under Gould's ownership. It was neither widely read nor generally respected. The fund drive was weakly promoted and was conducted on a small scale. It drew relatively few contributions. Preoccupied by his other pressing problems, Pulitzer soon dropped the Statue campaign—temporarily. When he picked it up again nearly two years later, the results would be dramatic.

But at the time when Pulitzer turned aside from the Statue, the committee's prospects looked bleaker than ever. Not only was the fund drive still faltering, but the news from Paris threatened new embarrassments.

In August 1883 Bartholdi reported to Richard Butler that work on the Statue was rapidly nearing completion. "We are," the sculptor wrote, "now raising the head [onto the body]. . . ."

Bartholdi's letter also conveyed his grief over the recent death of Laboulaye: "I would have been so gratified to see him sharing our satisfaction in the completion of the work to which he had shown such devotion."

Toward the end of the year the committee received formal notice from the French-American Union that the Statue was finished. The union awaited only the word from America that the pedestal was ready to receive it. In the meantime the Lady would keep her torch raised high above the rooftops of Paris. Thousands of French citizens and foreign tourists came streaming to the workshop every day to marvel at her.

The committee did come up with an intriguing idea which, it hoped, might breathe new life into the sluggish fund drive. It would assemble a collection of rare and precious art objects borrowed from wealthy private collectors, and would place them on public exhibition. Paintings, tapestries, Tiffany stained-glass windows, rugs, gold and silver objects of many types, were among the art works to be brought together. Most of them had never before been available for public showing. The committee was convinced that this unique collection would be impressive enough to draw large crowds. The entry fees would help fill the committee's sagging coffers.

The Bartholdi Statue Pedestal Fund Art Loan Exhibition opened at the National Academy of Design on December 4, 1883. It ran for four weeks, and it was an encouraging success. Some forty thousand visitors thronged to see it. The committee earned a net profit of $12,000.

This was certainly helpful, but it was very far from solving the committee's ever-threatening shortage of funds. Two days after the exhibition closed a committee spokesman admitted to the press, "We need $175,000 to $200,000 more to complete the pedestal."

6

THE LADY GETS A HEART

"Until we are all free, we are none of us free."
— Emma Lazarus, 1882

The Pedestal Fund Art Loan Exhibition produced another, very different, entirely unexpected result.

It happened when the committee decided to run a literary auction in connection with the exhibition. Members of the committee contacted the nation's leading authors and asked them to write something appropriate to the occasion. These manuscripts would then be auctioned off for the benefit of the pedestal fund.

The response was heartening. Celebrated authors who contributed their works included Mark Twain, Walt Whitman, and Bret Harte. The heirs of such recently deceased notables as Henry Wadsworth Longfellow and William Cullen Bryant donated selections by those writers.

There was a piece of writing by another author. She was a thirty-four-year-old poet, playwright, and essayist. Her writings had won the esteem of literary critics, of serious readers, and of some of the most respected writers of that era. But she was not yet so well-known as the others invited to contribute to the auction.

She was Emma Lazarus, and in time her name would be inseparably linked with the Statue. She would endow the Lady with a profound and poignant new meaning, radically different from what the original sponsors, and even Bartholdi himself, had in mind. Her impassioned words would change forever how the world thought and felt about the Statue.

Emma Lazarus was descended from one of the first Jewish families to emigrate from Europe to America, arriving in the mid-1600s. A later generation of her ancestors actively supported the American Revolution.

Emma Lazarus's father was a prosperous New York sugar refiner. She was brought up in an environment of comfort and culture. Like most upper-class young ladies of her time, she was educated by private tutors and lived a sheltered life.

Shy and serious minded in her youth, Lazarus preferred books and solitude to socializing. She was only sixteen when her first book of poems was published. William Cullen Bryant was one of those who praised her work as remarkable for one so young. Lazarus's writings also came to the attention of Ralph Waldo Emerson. The renowned New England poet-philosopher befriended the young writer and was for some years her mentor and idol.

Lazarus subsequently published several volumes of poetry, a drama in verse, a novel, and various other prose works. Her sensitive translations of the distinguished German poet Heinrich Heine are still classed among the finest ever achieved.

The themes Lazarus touched on in her writings were mostly of a universal nature. Only occasionally did she manifest a special interest in the history and culture of her own people. She had not received much of a religious education. Her parents attended their local temple only on the major holidays. Dr. Gustav Gottheil, rabbi at that temple, tried to interest the young Emma in Judaism. He did get her to translate a few hymns from the German.

She wrote him to apologize for "my own ignorance" in these matters. "All I can say . . . is that I am willing to learn, and always grateful to be taught the truth." A few weeks later she wrote again to assure him that "my interest and sympathies" are with the Jews, "although my religious convictions (if such they can be called) and the circumstances of my life have led me somewhat apart from our people."

Then, starting in 1879 and continuing for nearly five years, a wave of anti-Jewish violence swept across Russia and eastern Europe. Thousands were killed and maimed in these pogroms (organized mob attacks), which were either ignored or secretly encouraged by the Russian government. Other thousands managed to escape to America.

Americans were shocked and outraged by these mass killings. There were public protests and mass meetings. Former president U. S. Grant was among those who spoke out against the massacres of innocent people. For Emma Lazarus, it was the beginning of a deep personal transformation.

She attended one public meeting at which the main speaker was William M. Evarts, chairman of the American Committee for the Statue. He delivered a ringing denunciation of the pogroms. When Lazarus was introduced to him, she told him how much she had been stirred by his eloquence. It turned out that Evarts was an admirer of her writings—a fact that was soon to have fateful consequences.

In 1881, increasingly aroused by the persecution of her people, Lazarus broke out of her usual reserve and involved herself in the fate of the refugees now thronging to America's shores. She, who had for so long kept herself aloof from life's grimmer realities, visited the newcomers. Her first encounter with them was at Castle Garden, the reception center at the southern tip of Manhattan. Afterward she inspected the makeshift quarters that had been set up for them on Ward's Island, in the East River.

Lazarus had somehow assumed that the refugees would all be of the lower classes, ignorant, illiterate, thoroughly degraded by their long oppression under the hostile rule of Russia's czars. She was astounded to discover university graduates, talented professionals, and scholars among them. Particularly moving to her was the way the refugees gratefully performed whatever menial jobs might be asked of them while they awaited admission to the new land of freedom.

The conditions she found on Ward's Island appalled her. The place was unsanitary, there was inadequate running water, and the only available shelter was too flimsy for the coming winter. A riot had recently broken out among the seven hundred men, women, and children on the island because they were not receiving enough food to live on. Most of them had been stripped of all their possessions before being allowed to leave Russia.

Lazarus made herself into a forceful advocate for the refugees. She volunteered to assist in the work of the

Emma Lazarus, author of "The New Colossus."

Hebrew Emigrant Aid Society, and fought hard for immigrant relief. She helped establish New York's Hebrew Technical Institute, which provided the often unskilled refugees with badly needed vocational training.

Her sympathies extended to all who suffered. She was overwhelmed with emotion on reading *Progress and Poverty,* a book by the radical reformer Henry George. It contained vivid depictions of the wretched conditions under which the poor struggled to exist. It inspired her to write a poem smoldering with indignation, which was published in the *New York Times*. George wrote to thank her. She replied: "No person who prizes justice or common honesty can dine or sleep or read or work in peace until the monstrous wrong in which we are all accomplices is done away with."

Lazarus's commitment was tested anew in April 1882. An article by a Russian aristocrat, Mme. Zinaida A. Ragozin, appeared in a leading American literary periodical, *Century* magazine. A recognized historian and member of several learned societies in Europe, Mme. Ragozin took it upon herself to defend and "explain" the pogroms. They were really all the fault of the Jews, said Mme. Ragozin. Those who attacked them could hardly be blamed for defending themselves against Jewish exploitation and dishonesty. Mme. Ragozin later helped create one of the most notorious of all anti-Semitic forgeries, *The Protocols of the Elders of Zion*.

Lazarus replied in devastating terms in the next month's *Century*. She traced the long and bloody history of anti-Semitism, exposing and condemning those who had tolerated it through the centuries. She denounced not only the persecution of the Jews but persecutions of all kinds and against all peoples. "Until we are all free," she concluded, "we are none of us free."

Even before the pogroms, Lazarus had started a blank-verse drama about a harrowing example of anti-Jewish violence during the late Middle Ages. Titled *The Dance of Death,* it was the story of the execution of an entire village of Jews charged by their superstitious German rulers with bringing on an epidemic of bubonic plague. Movingly told in personal terms, seething with deeply felt rage and compassion, the play stood starkly apart from the genteel writings then customarily expected from lady poets.

Lazarus had withheld the completed work until she felt the time was ripe for its release. She now had it published serially in a monthly called the *American Hebrew*. Later in 1882 the play was issued, along with her translations of several ancient Hebrew poems, in a book which she proudly entitled *Songs of a Semite*. It was the first of her works to attain wide popular success.

In the course of her intimate contact with the refugees, Lazarus became aware that there remained many thousands who could not make it all the way to America. They needed a haven somewhere else. Ten years before the birth of the official Zionist movement, Lazarus became one of the first to advocate a Jewish homeland in Palestine.

She spent several months in Europe during 1883. Soon after her return, she had a visit from Evarts. He explained to her about the literary auction being held by the committee in connection with the Pedestal Fund Art Loan Exhibition. Would she write something that could be offered at the auction? With her growing reputation, such a manuscript might bring a respectable sum.

Her first response was negative; as a serious author she couldn't possibly "write verses to order." Evarts pointed out to her that the Lady's torch would shine with special brightness for the refugees from Russia. Lazarus was visibly moved, but she still felt unable to fulfill his request. Disappointed, Evarts took his leave.

But Lazarus could not get the idea out of her mind. For all those masses of poor immigrants arriving in ever-mounting numbers, the Statue as it loomed up over the horizon before their incoming ships would be their first experience of America and all it stood for. Perhaps she could find some way to speak to them in the Lady's own voice. Perhaps she could find words that would ease their painful passage from the familiar world they had left behind to this strange new world. Perhaps she could bid them a welcome worthy of America.

She got to work. She experimented with various forms. Finally she determined to cast the work in the classic shape of a sonnet. Always extremely meticulous in her writing, she was accustomed to revising and re-revising virtually every sentence until she could polish the words and phrases no more. This time, her pen almost seemed to find its own way across the page. Within a few hours, it was done.

THE NEW COLOSSUS

Not like the brazen giant of Greek fame,
With conquering limbs astride from land to land;
Here at our sea-washed, sunset gates shall stand
A mighty woman with a torch, whose flame
Is the imprisoned lightning, and her name
Mother of Exiles. From her beacon-hand
Glows world-wide welcome; her mild eyes command
The air-bridged harbor that twin cities frame.

"Keep, ancient lands, your storied pomp!" cries she
With silent lips. "Give me your tired, your poor,
Your huddled masses yearning to breathe free,
The wretched refuse of your teeming shore.
Send these, the homeless, tempest-tost to me.
I lift my lamp beside the golden door!"

Exhausted but satisfied, she sent the finished sonnet off to Evarts, and turned her attention to other matters.

Rarely if ever did Lazarus talk to anyone about the poem during the pitifully few remaining years of her life (stricken with cancer, she died in 1887 at the age of thirty-eight). She seems to have remained modestly unaware of the power of her work. Certainly she never imagined either its enduring impact or its worldwide fame. Even though the Statue was completed and officially dedicated in the year before her death, she apparently never visited it.

Only a select few recognized the poem's true worth during her lifetime. One of these was the poet and diplomat James Russell Lowell, who had long been a staunch admirer of Lazarus's work. He wrote her from England, where he was serving as U.S. ambassador:

> I must write again to say how much I like your sonnet about the Statue . . . [which] gives its subject a *raison d'être* [reason for being] which it wanted before quite as much as it wants a pedestal. You have set it upon a noble one, saying admirably just the right word to be said, an achievement more arduous than that of the sculptor.

Lowell added that he was working on a sonnet himself, and "I know how difficult a material one has to work in . . . [especially] when the subject is prescribed [by others] and not chosen."

More typical is the obituary which appeared in the *New York Times* on the day after Lazarus's death. The notice ran a respectful three-quarters of a column. It cited several of her writings, heaping praise upon them. The highest encomium was reserved for *Songs of a Semite,* which, said the *Times,* "ring with indignation against the belated prejudices that remain over the past among our worst heritages of bigotry."

But the *Times* writer had apparently never heard of "The New Colossus." Nowhere in the obituary is Lazarus's masterpiece even mentioned.

In 1903, the sonnet was enshrined on a bronze plaque affixed inside the Statue's pedestal. For some time the authorities were mystified as to the origin of this plaque. The National Park Service, which today has jurisdiction over the Statue, has no official record of its source.

The most generally accepted opinion at first was that Lazarus's family had placed it there. Ultimately, it was learned that a descendant of one of New York's oldest and wealthiest families, an artist and patron of the arts named Georgianna Schuyler, was responsible. She had been moved to correct what seemed to her an injustice, for neither Emma Lazarus nor her poem had previously received any form of official recognition.

Gradually but surely, the poem won its way to public affection. The original sponsors' intentions for the Statue slowly faded out before the brilliance of Emma Lazarus's new concept of the Lady—and hence of America—as the welcoming "Mother of Exiles."

History very quickly proved that Lazarus's sonnet had been inspired by a prophetic vision. Its writing coincided with the beginning of the greatest wave of immigration in America's history. In 1886, the year of the Statue's dedication, almost three hundred fifty thousand immigrants entered the United States. By 1903, and for a dozen years thereafter, the average number of arrivals each year was about one million.

The rising tide of immigration produced a backlash of suspicion and resentment among some segments of the native-born American population. Most of the newcomers were from eastern and southern Europe. That area had not previously supplied any significant part of the nation's ethnic makeup. In their appearance, language, customs, religion, their whole style of life, the new immigrants seemed different from the American majority. Most arrived in a state of abject poverty. They had few skills and little education. They seemed willing to accept the most menial kinds of work and the lowest wages.

Before they could be admitted to the United States, most of these immigrants had to be processed at a big new reception center on Ellis Island. Its location in New York harbor was not far from the Statue site on Bedloe's Island.

It was not long before a movement arose aimed at reducing the tremendous inflow. The new immigrants were increasingly looked on as potential bearers of dangerous or even revolutionary political and social ideas. The first law designed to restrict immigration from southern and eastern Europe was passed by the Congress in 1915. President Wilson, who believed the eager immigrants would strengthen the nation rather than weaken it, vetoed the proposal. He vetoed another such bill in 1917, but this time the Congress passed it over his veto. Even more restrictive laws were passed in 1921 and 1924, and the flood of immigrants quickly shrank to a trickle.

The exuberant welcome of Emma Lazarus's sonnet had been virtually silenced.

Not until after World War II did the nation begin to have second thoughts about its attitudes toward exiles. Americans by that time were becoming aware of the many-faceted immigrant contribution to the nation's way of life—including the immigrants' share in the victories in both world wars.

The new feeling was manifested in the 1950s by a movement favoring the establishment of an American Museum of Immigration on Bedloe's Island, at the base of the Statue. President Dwight D. Eisenhower lent his support when the proponents of this idea came to see him in 1954. On the Statue's seventy-fifth anniversary in 1961, the museum's cornerstone was laid. The mayor of Paris attended.

Four years later, the Congress passed and President Lyndon B. Johnson signed a liberalized new immigration law, reopening Emma Lazarus's "golden door."

The immigration museum was completed in 1972. Its exhibits explained, illustrated, and dramatized the many roles immigrants had played in building the American nation. Private citizens had contributed $2 million toward its construction; the federal government gave $5 million.

Emma Lazarus's song was once again heard in the land, clear and unmuffled.

Over the years the originally ignored sonnet has received its full measure of acclaim. Literary critics and historians alike have analyzed it and sought to explain its haunting eloquence. Generations of schoolchildren have memorized and recited it, especially those resounding last five lines.

But most immigrants no longer sail past the Statue as they arrive in New York. To bring the sonnet more into touch with modern realities, its last five lines have been inscribed on the wall of the International Arrivals Building at New York's John F. Kennedy International Airport.

The poem has even been set to music. One such occasion was a musical comedy about the Statue which opened on Broadway in 1949, entitled *Miss Liberty.* Its score was composed by Irving Berlin, creator of dozens of America's perennial popular songs. He gave the sonnet a stately musical setting, with a chorus of fifty-five singing it in the show's grand finale. A drama critic called this "one of the great moments on Broadway." The composer gave all his royalties to charity. Whenever possible, it is still performed at the Statue's anniversary celebrations.

Perhaps the most appropriate summation of the poem's significance was penned by Eve Merriam, a poet and playwright who wrote a biography of Emma Lazarus in the 1950s. The sonnet, said Merriam, "gave the Statue a human heart."

But we have gotten ahead of our story. Back in 1883, when Lazarus created the sonnet, it was still far from certain that funds sufficient to finance the pedestal would ever be raised.

7
THE LADY IS EMBARRASSED

If we could manage to have the ship bearing [the Statue] sunk in mid-ocean, we would be spared the humiliation of receiving this magnificent gift before we had even provided a place for it to stand on.
— Editorial in the *Chicago News,* 1885

The Lady's future certainly looked bleak in 1883, but it was not hopeless. The committee had accumulated at least enough money to start construction.

Work would proceed in four phases. The first step was to dig the huge excavation that would contain the foundation. Tons of concrete would then be poured to form the foundation. Only then could the pedestal be erected. Finally, the Lady herself would assume her rightful place as the crowning element.

Contracts for the excavation were let in March 1883. Ground was broken the following month. General Stone, the former U.S. Army commander now in charge of construction, issued the first in what was to become a series of overoptimistic predictions. The pedestal, he told the press, would be finished by the summer of 1884. The Statue would be in place that fall. He was wrong by almost exactly two years.

The excavation job proved more difficult, and considerably more expensive, than expected. The workmen discovered that Fort Wood, built before the War of 1812, had been erected on top of much older fortifications of extremely sturdy masonry, probably constructed by the Dutch. These would have to be cleared away before work could proceed. The ramparts of the fort itself, which in the general's words consisted "of blocks of [granite] well laid," would be allowed to stand.

After six months of grueling toil, the excavation reached its full depth of over thirty feet. Actual pouring of the concrete foundation inside it began in October. The foundation built up gradually. When it was finished eight months later, it was the largest concrete block in existence.

The huge mass, unchanged ever since, takes the form of a stepped pyramid tapering from ninety-one feet square at the bottom to sixty-seven feet square at the top. It has a total depth of fifty-three feet, of which twenty-two feet rise above the fortress walls. It contains some twelve thousand cubic feet of concrete.

Running through the center from top to bottom is an open shaft ten feet square, designed to accommodate an elevator. Two arched passageways run through it at ground level, meeting at the center.

Samples taken from the foundation and tested in 1885 showed that it could resist crushing forces of from 72 to 131 tons on each square foot. The actual pressure at the bottom of the foundation, with both pedestal and Statue bearing down upon it, is a mere 5 tons to the square foot. Miss Liberty stands upon solid footing indeed.

It is amusing to see what has happened to an above-ground section of the foundation, which is exposed to view as part of the exhibit in the museum at the base of the Statue. Visitors have taken to tossing coins onto the steps that form the stepped pyramid. Some seem to do it just for good luck. Others compete to see who can get their coins to land—and stay—on the highest of the narrow steps. On a busy day, the section gleams with pennies, nickels, dimes, quarters—and an assortment of odd objects.

The foundation cost almost $94,000. Announcing its completion, the ever-optimistic General Stone declared that enough money remained for a good start on the pedestal. Committee treasurer Spaulding hastily amended the general's statement, pointing out that the pedestal would require at least $100,000 more than the Committee had.

In March 1884 a letter came in to the committee that offered tempting financial help—but it was a kind of help that could not even be considered. An official of the Centaur Company proposed to make a donation of $25,000. This would have been by far the largest contribution received to date. The only condition was that a huge sign advertising the company's product, Castoria (a widely used children's laxative), be placed atop the pedestal at the Statue's feet for a full year. The offer was, of course, refused.

Even in that rough-and-tumble era in the history of American business, the Castoria offer stood out for its sheer crassness. But it was only an early example of the many attempts to exploit the Statue for profit that have taken place since then.

Meanwhile, construction proceeded. Before long Bedloe's Island acquired a tiny railroad. It would carry the newly quarried granite for the pedestal from the boat to the construction site. The builders also purchased a ferryboat to shuttle supplies from the mainland. She was ceremoniously christened the *Bartholdi,* and began regular trips on July 20, 1884.

Two weeks later a small but dignified ceremony marked the laying of the pedestal's cornerstone. A copper box placed inside it contained copies of the Declaration of Independence and the Constitution, the daily newspapers, a history of the Statue and a history of the Brooklyn Bridge (completed the previous year), some coins, and other historic memorabilia.

Despite these signs of progress, the money problem would not go away. The Statue fund had risen to $150,000 by then, but almost all of this amount had either been spent or committed for upcoming expenses. The committee could only cast desperately about for new ways to raise funds.

At this point, the first truly national organization to volunteer its aid to the cause came forward. The Sons of the American Revolution, a patriotic body with branches throughout the country, issued a "Call for Subscriptions to the Pedestal Fund of the Statue of Liberty."

The "call" noted that the committee only had funds for "18 working days longer." Pedestal construction expenses amounted to $300 a day. No less than $125,000 was needed to finish the job.

"The disgrace would be national," said this nationwide appeal, if the work were brought to a standstill for lack of funds. This would be "particularly galling to every American possessed of the least feeling of patriotism." Americans could not leave it to "a few rich men." Every man, woman, and child "should have a block in the pedestal."

The Sons of the American Revolution announced that the steamboat *Florence* would shortly begin regular runs between New York and Bedloe's Island. Tickets were twenty-five cents, with the receipts going to the Statue fund. Donors responding to the call would receive free boat tickets in proportion to their donations.

The patriotic organization even sponsored a big fund-raising rally in the heart of New York's financial district. There were speakers, a band, and a big sign urging passersby to contribute the "1,250,000 ten-cent pieces" that were needed for the pedestal.

Hope ran high at the committee for these welcome efforts. Sadly, the results proved disappointing. The Sons of the American Revolution brought in a little more than two thousand dollars—a helpful contribution but no more than a small dent in the massive deficit.

All this while, Bartholdi kept trying to be helpful. Early in 1884 he painstakingly wrote out his signature three thousand times and mailed the autographs to the committee, for sale to souvenir hunters. They proved quite popular.

In a letter to a friend, the sculptor explained why he felt it necessary to go to such lengths: "In all matters affecting public opinion, someone has to blow on the fire; it's often hard work, but the result is satisfying."

By that time the committee's funds were being used up with dismaying rapidity as construction progressed. The members had to give up on their oft-repeated pledge to raise all necessary moneys from private sources. They would have to get help from the government.

They turned first to New York City. Its officials were sympathetic, since the Statue would benefit the city in many ways. But under the law the city could help fi-

The Wall Street rally staged by the Sons of the American Revolution to aid the lagging fund drive for the pedestal, probably in 1884.

nance a privately sponsored enterprise only if the state granted permission. The Statue's friends in the state legislature promptly introduced a bill authorizing aid to the Statue in the amount of $50,000. The bill passed both houses of the legislature without difficulty. There remained only the required signature of the governor.

New York's governor at that time was Grover Cleveland, the future two-term president. To the committee's surprise and consternation, Cleveland vetoed the bill. He pointed out that the state constitution forbade any municipality from spending public funds for private undertakings.

Ironically, the governor who vetoed this desperately needed aid was to be a proud guest of honor—as president—at the great ceremony of October 28, 1886, celebrating the Statue's unveiling.

If neither the city nor the state would help, perhaps the federal government could be persuaded. Members of the committee contacted their congressmen. Their influence produced a bill to grant $100,000 for the Statue's remaining costs. It was passed by both houses of Congress as part of a more general appropriations bill. President Chester A. Arthur favored it.

But there were differences between the House and Senate versions. In the negotiations to resolve these differences, the appropriation for the Statue was mysteriously dropped. It may have been forced out by representatives from states which felt that New York alone should pay these costs. Or it may have been defeated on the same grounds as before: The use of public funds for a private project was thought to constitute a dangerous precedent.

The disappointed committee could only search anxiously for new fund-raising ideas. The *Times* had a suggestion. It noted that Hunt's design for the pedestal called for it to be ornamented with an array of forty large granite medallions, one for each state admitted to the Union so far.

"Each State of the Union," the *Times* proposed, "should now vote a round sum to the fund and have its shield artistically engraved on the monument." This seemingly reasonable idea, like others designed to bring in revenue from outside New York, probably ran afoul of the anti–New York feeling that was still widespread at that time. There was no response from the other states. The medallions remain blank to this day.

By the end of November 1884, funds on hand were so low that work on the pedestal had to be suspended. It had reached a height of only fifteen feet, with nearly seventy-five feet still to be built.

Once again, New York's difficulties prompted other cities to covet the Statue. On December 4, 1884, it was the *Baltimore American* testing the possibilities: "New York clearly does not deserve the Statue. Baltimore will welcome it proudly and gladly."

And once again it was George Jones of the *New York Times* unleashing his sarcasm at the presumptuous would-be raiders. If such a town as Baltimore could contend for the Statue, Jones sneered, then why not such equally estimable villages as Painted Post, New York, or Glover, Vermont? Jones declared his preference for Glover. Its population was at least as worthy as that of Baltimore—even though it numbered only 1,178.

San Francisco entered the competition a few days later. Its leading newspaper, the *Bulletin,* boastfully proclaimed the city's readiness to assume all costs. And besides, San Francisco could offer a site as beautifully suited to the spirit of the Statue as New York harbor:

> We will engage to set it up on Telegraph Hill without expense to anyone. Upon that great natural pediment it will face the great Pacific Ocean and forever hold up its torch to enlighten the enslaved millions of the oldest section of the world beyond.

This time, Jones and the *Times* chose simply to ignore the challenge.

But some facts could not be ignored. Dismantled in January 1885 for shipment to the United States, the Statue would soon be on its way aboard the French warship *Isère.*

The committee's dismay grew more intense with every passing day. Work on the pedestal, halted in November for lack of funds, remained in suspension as the months rolled by. New contributions were scarcely dribbling in. From December 1, 1884, to March 10, 1885, they totaled less than $16,000. It was beginning to look as if the Lady might never find a home in America.

· 8 ·
THE LADY CONQUERS AMERICA

Stone by stone, no more to stop,
Freedom's throne is builded up;
Upward goes the granite gray,
Still it grows with every day.
Still they come like drops of rain,
Every sum a welcome gain.
Roll the ball, and still it grows,
One and all—and up she goes!
— A *New York World* reader, 1886

Just as things were at their blackest, a ray of hope broke through the gloom.

Joseph Pulitzer, publisher of the *New York World,* had grown increasingly furious over the Statue's money woes. On March 14, 1885, he published an editorial titled "The National Disgrace." As he had done during his first campaign for the Statue two years earlier, he blasted away at the "millionaires who would expend thousands on a foreign singer or ballet dancer and pour out their money lavishly in aping aristocratic follies." These same individuals, Pulitzer stormed, "are too penurious and too unpatriotic to contribute a dollar towards a pedestal. . . ."

Two days later he launched a new fund-raising effort.

In a second editorial he pledged all his resources to avoid "the irrevocable disgrace" of having the soon-to-arrive Statue stored away in some warehouse because there was no pedestal for it. The *World* would single-handedly raise the $100,000 needed to finish the job.

> The *World* is the people's paper, and it now appeals to the people to come forward and raise this money. The $250,000 that the Statue cost was paid in by the masses of the French people—by the working-men, the tradesmen, the shop girls, the artisans—by all irrespective of class or condition. Let us respond in like manner. Let us not wait for the millionaires to give this money. It is not a gift from the millionaires of France to the millionaires of America, but a gift of the whole people of France to the whole people of America.

Pulitzer pleaded with his readers to "give something, however little." He concluded with an idea that turned out to be one of the most effective fund-raising gimmicks ever: "We will . . . publish the name of every giver, however small the sum given."

Pulitzer's decision to rejoin the crusade was the best news the despairing committee had heard in many months. In the relatively short time since his purchase of the *World,* Pulitzer had transformed it into the nation's most widely read newspaper. Its circulation had reached the then unheard-of figure of one hundred sixty thousand. The potential benefits to the Lady's fortunes were dizzying.

Seeing their names in print may not have been the only factor that persuaded tens of thousands to contribute, but it proved to be a powerful enticement. Public response to the *World*'s new drive exceeded all expectations. In pennies and dimes and dollars, the ordinary working people of New York and the nation gave solid evidence of their growing affection for the Statue. More than $2,000 poured in during the first week.

So touching were many of the letters that the *World* published them along with the names of their authors. They helped stimulate donations then, and they make poignant reading today.

"I am a young girl alone in the world, and earning my own living," wrote one humble donor. "Enclosed please find 60 cents, the result of self-denial. I wish I could make it 60 thousand dollars instead of cents, but drops make the ocean. . . ."

A donor describing himself as "a cash boy with a salary of $5.00 per month" sent 50 cents. A "poor office boy" could offer only a nickel. A ten-year-old girl sent "my pocket-piece—20 cents in silver." A gift of $1 came from "a lonely and very aged woman."

Jane M. wrote that she was "only a sewing girl, but I am in full sympathy with your effort." She managed to spare 50 cents from her tiny weekly wage.

Such small donations may seem absurd by today's standards. But every penny of that era was worth perhaps fifty times as much in today's inflated currency.

Then as now, the nation's schools responded eagerly to a patriotic cause. Collections taken in the twelve public schools of Trenton, New Jersey, yielded $105.07. The teachers and pupils of the New York Institute for the Instruction of the Deaf and Dumb sent $10.40. All the way from Davenport, Iowa, a kindergarten class mailed in its carefully collected gift of $1.35. The children of a public school in Arlington, New Jersey, had set up a collection box in their classroom. Their pennies gradually mounted to a grand total of $3.52, which they proudly gave.

A single day brought contributions from fifteen hundred public-school children; the next day offerings were received from a thousand more. New York City's Catholic schools gave generously. Columbia College students ran a highly profitable fund drive on campus.

Younger children were not to be outdone. Helen and Milton Samek gave $1, "the contents of our little savings bank, which we cheerfully contribute." Nina, Maria, and Antoinette of Irvington-on-Hudson, New York, "asked mamma and pappa to let us send you money . . . so we decided to open the toy bank in our dolls' house, and we send you some."

The children of one family said they had taken three lessons in French "and we don't like it, but we love the good French people for giving us this beautiful Statue and we send you $1, the money we have saved to go to the circus with."

Young Addie M. Berryman too had reason for pride:

> We are fourteen little boys and girls and we made up a club for the Pedestal Fund and I hope our pennies will do some good. Instead of spending our money for candy we saved up. I made up this letter myself. I am the president.

Like today's youngsters responding to a charity telethon, children of that era were willing fund-raisers for a cause they believed in. A typical letter ran: "I am a little boy eleven years old, and enclose $3, which I have collected in small sums. I hope every little boy will do the same." Two others wrote: "When we get to be big men we want to say we helped to build the Pedestal. . . . So we started out to raise money and we now send you $13. Maybe we will have more."

Veterans of the Union Army were another fertile source. New York's own Seventh Regiment had contributed $1,500 to the *World*'s first campaign of 1883. For the second one two years later, the regiment ran a giant entertainment which brought in thousands more. Other military units were equally generous.

The Revolutionary War too brought its legacy. An offering of 50 cents came from "a lad whose great-grandfather fought side by side with Lafayette for our liberties." R. W. Gaffney wrote that his great-grandfather too had " 'fit in the Revolution,' and I feel mighty kind to the French." His gift was $1.

A "young man of foreign birth" gave as his reason for contributing that he had "seen enough of monarchical governments to appreciate the blessings of this republic." He sent $2.

Another immigrant, Ferdinand Lemoine, could not understand why more Americans did not contribute: "I have been born in France but I am citizen of this country 22 years. I feel ashamed when I think of the indifference of Americans to the gift of my native land." He sent $1.

An immigrant's son was sorry that he could send only 25 cents. But he expressed a feeling shared by many of the newcomers' descendants: "I think it is the duty of every man whose father came up through the Narrows to this glorious country to do likewise."

The fund-raising campaign may have helped lower the level of drunkenness in Brooklyn, at least temporarily. No less than $15—then a considerable sum—was received from "some of the inmates of the Inebriates' [Alcoholics'] Home of Kings County." For others who drank, collection boxes were set up in bars and saloons all over town.

Local poker clubs proved an unexpected source. The Robinson Crusoe Club of Jersey City, New Jersey, reported that it had set aside a "Poker Widow" fund at its Friday-night game. Five cents was deducted from every jackpot. Total donation: $1.50. The Ten O'Clock Poker Club sent in "the contents of the first jackpot" of the evening, which came to $4.

One young lady, thinking perhaps of the delicate imported material of her fine gloves, wrote: "As 'French kid' [leather] is peculiarly liable to damage from water, please accept my mite . . . towards providing dry footing for Mlle. Liberty."

There were also some joke contributions. One letter pretended to bear the signatures of two of the wealthiest business tycoons of that era, William H. Vanderbilt and Jay Gould. "Please find enclosed $500," it ran, "and don't fail to acknowledge same in your columns, so that we may no longer be called the 'Close-fisted millionaires.' " The donation was in Confederate currency.

A group of workers, "poor in pocket but rich in patriotism," sent in the $7.50 they had painstakingly accumulated over the course of many weeks.

Not all the donations arrived in pennies. The *World* itself gave $1,000 to get things started. A collection taken on the floor of the New York Stock Exchange yielded a check for the same amount. Jersey City's Pierre Lorillard, of the wealthy tobacco family, sent another $1,000.

But in general the wealthier classes ignored the campaign. Many disliked the *World* because it was a Democratic newspaper, while they were mostly Republicans. Others seemed to feel more suspicion than sympathy for a monument symbolizing the revolutionary ideal of liberty.

The *World* kept hammering away at the resistance of the rich. One editorial read:

> The rich men of the country still manifest their indifference, but the People are moving. The sons of toil, the little schoolchildren, the shop-girls, the ragged newsboys, the wage-workers—all who have reason to know the value of Liberty—are sending their pennies, their dimes, and even their dollars. . . . Mr. Vanderbilt may not contribute of his great means, but the employees of Mr. Vanderbilt's railways—the section hands and trackmen, who work for slender wages—have sent $60.

One *World* reader responded: "I am a poor man or I would send more than the enclosed 10 cents. . . . You go right on, Mr. World, and make it hot for the nobs and snobs!"

The letters and lists of donors soon developed into a daily feature occupying almost an entire page. They ran under the banner heading, "The *World*'s Bartholdi Pedestal Fund," with a sketch of Uncle Sam, hat in hand, begging for donations in front of the Statue.

Influenced by the *World*'s well-publicized success, others now bestirred themselves on the fund's behalf. A popular actor named Robert B. Mantell gave a series of dramatic recitals. The newspaper reported that "the sporting fraternity" had arranged "an athletic and boxing entertainment." The Brighton Beach Association gave a racing benefit. Contributions flowed in from as far away as California, Colorado, Florida, Louisiana.

The *World*'s big push moved donors to give directly to the committee as well. Many came to committee headquarters during these months, signed a book that was kept there, and wrote in the amount of their donation. Besides the many New Yorkers there were donors from Des Moines; Jacksonville; St. Louis; San Francisco; Fort Smith, Arkansas; San Mateo, California; Waco, Texas—as well as England, Ireland, Scotland, France, Italy, and Cuba.

Newspapers elsewhere joined the fight. Pulitzer's own *St. Louis Post-Dispatch* was of course in the forefront, exhorting its readers to help. It eventually collected over $1,600. The *Philadelphia Press,* the *New Haven Register,* the Washington, D.C., newspapers, all added their voices. Praise and good wishes filled editorials in the *Boston Transcript,* the *Pittsburgh Dispatch,* the *Cleveland Leader,* the *Baltimore American,* and newspapers in Jacksonville, Milwaukee, and Cincinnati. Even the once skeptical *New York Times* commended the *World* and chipped in $250.

The *Ottumwa* (Iowa) *Democrat* made a caustic point in an editorial: "The New York *World* Pedestal Fund has reached $6,000. The Vanderbilt tomb is to cost $200,000. The price of one Vanderbilt is about 30 Liberty Pedestals."

Only a few weeks earlier, most Americans were still thinking of the Statue's financial problems as a dilemma affecting only New Yorkers. Now it was becoming a national crusade. The Lady was winning the heart of America.

Pulitzer had placed one of his most experienced reporters, John R. Reavis, in charge of the fund drive. Reavis devoted himself to it totally, enthusiastically, and effectively. Pulitzer rewarded him with a bonus and a raise in salary. As the amount collected mounted toward the goal, Reavis wrote to Pulitzer:

> I am glad of my success not only for my sake but for your sake, the paper's sake, and the sake of the country. . . . The heart of the people is with us and the people will stand by us and help us to the end. It is a grand thing to see a newspaper leading the sentiment of a nation.

By early April, with the fund level rising rapidly, the

committee ordered work resumed on granite quarrying and cutting. On May 11, construction crews got the green light to resume their labors on the pedestal itself.

On a single day in early June, the *World* received two contrasting donations. On the one hand there was the Union League Club, an elite organization that included some of the nation's wealthiest and most conservative individuals. It sent $2,000. On the other hand there was a donation of $10 which, the newspaper reported, "represents 1,000 contributors." It had come from the children of the Hebrew Free School Association. They each gave a penny a week to be used for charitable contributions. That week, they had asked that their pennies go to help build the pedestal.

Three days later the American committee ran a full-page ad in the *World* and many other newspapers. With Bartholdi's help and support, it had come up with a new fund-raising device. It offered a six-inch "Miniature Statuette," with the Statue "bronzed" and the pedestal "nickel-silvered." The price was $1. A twelve-inch version was available for $5.

These were the only authentic and fully detailed reproductions on the American market, said the ad. They were also protected by copyrights in the sculptor's name. Bartholdi would receive royalties rewarding him for his years of unpaid and selfless service on the Statue's behalf. The country's top retail firms had agreed to sell the copies, at no cost to the committee.

E. J. Layley, who was in charge of mail orders for these reproductions at the committee headquarters in New York, was interviewed on the Statue's fiftieth anniversary in 1936. "The largest size," he remembered, "was really an important souvenir, standing on a plush base, and was a favorite with the subscribers." Layley felt certain that "in many families the original statuettes were kept as heirlooms." Doubtless these meticulously produced miniatures are still cherished possessions in many American homes today.

They were so popular at the time that Layley had to put in many extra hours to keep up with the orders. When Bartholdi visited the committee offices, he was told of Layley's devoted service. Layley never forgot what happened next:

> He listened with courtesy and thanked me. . . . He took from his pocket a medal . . . showing an engraving of the Goddess of Liberty. It was attached to a tri-colored ribbon—the red, white, and blue of France. He pinned it to my lapel. I could not have been more thrilled if I had received the symbol of the Legion of Honor.

The *World* campaign had been under way for three months when it received another powerful boost. On June 17, after a stormy Atlantic crossing, the French warship *Isere* sailed proudly into New York harbor. Undamaged in her hold were the 214 crates containing the dismantled Statue.

New York greeted the momentous event with hastily mounted pomp. Representatives of the federal government, of New York State, and of the city sailed out to hail the *Isère* as she reached Bedloe's Island. The U.S. Navy's North Atlantic squadron escorted the French vessel through the harbor. Crowds estimated at two hundred thousand people jammed the waterfront. "Every species of craft known to the sea was in line for the *Isère*," the *Times* reported, "all flying the French flag." Naval and land-based artillery competed with ear-shattering salutes.

The city's downtown buildings were gaily bedecked

Sales of this model by the American Committee provided the only significant repayment Bartholdi ever received in his years of selfless devotion to the cause of the Statue.

with French and American flags. Huge crowds cheered a colorful parade that included several American regiments. New York's French units, the Gardes Lafayette and the Grenadiers Rochambeau, acted as the honor guard. Mayor William H. Grace delivered a welcoming address.

The Statue's arrival was headline news in most of the city's newspapers. Even the usually sedate *Times* was emblazoned with a front-page banner headline, "THE GREAT STATUE HERE." The *World*'s headline was "WELCOME, LIBERTY!"

Heartfelt and well-intentioned as the welcome was, it could not mask one unpleasant reality. As the *Isère* sailed past Bedloe's Island, every eye was inevitably drawn to the unfinished state of the pedestal.

But neither Americans nor Frenchmen were downcast. Donations were still pouring in. What the *World* called "the most noble band of more than 86,000 patriots" had already swelled the *World* fund to about $75,000. Work on the pedestal was moving forward as fast as it could be pushed. The Lady's home would soon be fit to receive her.

August 11 was the day of triumph. "ONE HUNDRED THOUSAND DOLLARS!" The *World* trumpeted its achievement with a banner headline and an enthusiastic front-page article, accompanied by a sketch of the Lady holding up the American flag beside her torch. A beaming Uncle Sam was shown completing an imaginary inscription on the pedestal: "This Pedestal of LIBERTY was provided by the Voluntary Contributions of 120,000 PATRIOTIC CITIZENS of the American Union through the NEW YORK WORLD. *Finis Coronat Opus* [literally, 'The End Crowns the Work']."

The whole whirlwind campaign had lasted just five months. The most remarkable fact about it is that eighty percent of the total was received in sums of less than one dollar.

· 9 ·

THE LADY MOUNTS HER PEDESTAL

We shall not forget that Liberty has here made her home; nor shall her chosen altar be neglected. . . . [Her] stream of light shall pierce the darkness of ignorance and man's oppression until Liberty enlightens the world.

—President Grover Cleveland at the dedication of the Statue of Liberty, October 28, 1886

Designing a pedestal for the most spectacular monument ever built was a fearsome challenge. The colossal size of the Statue demanded a pedestal that would be grandly impressive in and of itself. At the same time it must not distract from the Statue, but must remain subordinate to it. The pedestal must also look attractive in relation to the Fort Wood setting.

The earliest concept of the pedestal appeared in Bartholdi's watercolor sketch of 1871, his first visualization of the Statue on its Bedloe's Island site. He drew the pedestal as a hexagonal tower, looking very much like the keep of a medieval fortress.

Bartholdi was never quite satisfied with that design. Some time around 1880 he worked out an entirely different, more impressive layout. It called for a tremendous stepped pyramid, leading up to a low pedestal in the classical style. But this was still no more than a tentative idea. The final form of the pedestal remained an open question.

Richard Morris Hunt, the American architect appointed by the committee to work out the final design, was at first deeply impressed by Bartholdi's classical concept. Ultimately he concluded that it was unsuitable.

The sculptor's plan, Hunt felt, might have produced an excellent effect on any other site. But surrounded by the massive outward-thrusting walls of Fort Wood, he argued, Bartholdi's pyramid would look flat and uninspiring. The pedestal must instead counteract the horizontal spread of the fortress with a strong, dynamic, upward thrust. Hunt's solution differed drastically from Bartholdi's. As soon as he saw Hunt's first drawings of it, the sculptor quickly and generously admitted its superiority.

It did have one flaw, however; it was so tall that it almost seemed to belittle the Statue. Hunt agreed to reduce it to its present height of eighty-nine feet. The committee then gave its formal approval.

Hunt's revised design has won almost unanimous acclaim over the years. Its simple, square form is relieved of monotony by a Doric frieze, a triple balcony, and by the forty shields representing the states then in the Union. In addition, Hunt incorporated the decorative notion of having some of the granite blocks project slightly from the pedestal's surface, almost like a random checkerboard. The result is handsome, dignified, and perfectly matched to its role in relation to both the Statue and the site.

The pedestal walls are seventeen and a half feet thick

at the base, thinning gradually to a little over six feet at the top. They cover the foundation's sixty-five square feet, and then taper to forty-three square feet at the base of the Statue.

Only the exterior is of granite, with blocks that average three feet thick. The rest, for reasons of economy, is concrete. At the center is a vertical shaft twenty-seven feet square, which accommodates the elevator and various other facilities. A doorway in each of the pedestal's four faces leads through arched passageways to the central shaft.

Financial problems prevented installation of the elevator for over twenty years. Visitors in those early years had a considerably longer climb than do those of today.

Now that the *World*'s fund drive had succeeded, erection of the pedestal moved steadily to completion. The last concrete block was laid on April 22, 1886.

General Stone exulted that "not a man has been killed or injured" on the job. Considering its size and difficulty, this was an exceptional accomplishment. Looking at it another way, one might say that the Lady had been kind to her builders.

But even at that proud moment, neither the general nor the committee could escape the inexorable fact that still more money was needed—and the committee was broke.

The dismantled Statue and its interior support framework still had to be reassembled and erected on the pedestal. These jobs were expected to cost an additional $15,000 to $20,000. Until that amount had been raised no further progress was possible.

General Stone issued a statement to the newspapers asking "respectfully" that one or more wealthy individuals give the needed sum. They should do it out of "national feeling and civic pride." Compared to the nearly $300,000 already spent on the pedestal, it seemed a small amount.

Once again Bartholdi, never at a loss for new ideas, tried to help. He wrote to a member of the committee that the money might be raised "by borrowing the amount from some banker and giving a mortgage upon the product of the entrance fee. . . ." Bartholdi suggested charging 25 cents on weekdays and 10 cents on Sundays. The French committee had done this to cover the expenses incurred in finishing up the Statue. "We made in about four months more than 61,000 francs [about $15,000] clear profit."

If that were deemed inadvisable, the sculptor volunteered to come over "and deliver some lectures with electrical projections [slides]."

The committee doubtless discussed Bartholdi's ideas, but rejected the notion of charging a fee for visits to the Statue. Under the sponsorship of the federal government admission has been free ever since, though visitors do pay for the boat trip to the island.

Bartholdi's lecture tour could not be arranged either. Instead, renewed newspaper appeals and new fund-raising activities of various kinds were tried. The results were sparse.

The sculptor nevertheless found a way to contribute. He wrote a long essay recounting the Statue's entire history. It was published in the *North American Review,* a highly respected periodical. Bartholdi donated his fee to the Statue fund.

A "Prefatory Note" introducing the essay, written by one of the *Review*'s editors, summed up Bartholdi's life and career. It drew attention to the fact that Bartholdi had labored on this project for over ten years, "a labor of love and not of profit." Presumably the work was its own reward: "In consecrating a tribute to Liberty, he has fashioned the eighth wonder of the world."

Bartholdi's contribution of his fee for the essay, while accepted gratefully, still left the committee short of funds. Once again, the committee had to turn to the federal government.

President Cleveland was persuaded to send a special message to Congress. He asked for funds not only for setting up the Statue, but also for the now approaching dedication ceremony. After considerable squabbling, Congress passed a $56,500 appropriation. One of the bill's provisions banned the use of any of this money to purchase alcoholic beverages to be consumed at the dedication. The temperance movement was becoming increasingly influential.

Work could now be resumed. The first step was erecting Eiffel's iron pylon with its secondary armature. It was in place by early July. Then, at last, the first two of the Statue's copper plates were riveted to the iron strapwork. Bartholdi's name was engraved on the first of them, Pulitzer's on the second.

Some of the individually sculptured plates were found to have lost their precise original shape during the voyage. They had to be refitted, a painstaking and time-consuming task.

Slowly, as one after another of the copper plates was set in its proper location, the Lady began to reveal herself to the view of Americans for the first time. By the time she stood forth whole and complete, her noble form had required a total of three hundred thousand copper rivets. They are virtually invisible from the outside.

When the last rivet had been driven, Liberty towered nearly 306 feet from sea level to torch. She was the

Mounting the framework on the pedestal, while parts of the dismantled Statue wait on the ground.

world's tallest man-made structure. Her nearest rival in New York was the steeple of Trinity Church, at 286 feet. The great arched stone towers of the Brooklyn Bridge, completed just three years earlier and the sensation of their day, reached only 282 feet. Only the Eiffel Tower in Paris would stand taller during that era; but it was not erected until 1889.

Bartholdi had written to Hunt earlier that he was concerned about how the Statue was to be anchored to the pedestal. Considering New York harbor's frequent storms and high winds, this was obviously a crucial problem. Bartholdi urged Hunt to employ the most qualified people he could find to deal with it. Hunt worked with Eiffel to devise a flawless solution.

Hunt laid four massive steel beams just inside the bottom of the pedestal walls, and four more at the top. The upper and lower beams were connected by powerful steel girders running up along the inside of the walls.

Eiffel's pylon was then joined to both the upper and lower beams with enormous bolts. The result is a linkage so secure that, in the words of art historian Marvin Trachtenberg, "to overturn the Statue one would have to upturn the island itself."

The exact placement of the pedestal and Statue had caused Bartholdi serious concern. He had at first imagined the Lady facing toward the harbor entrance at the Narrows, and toward the Atlantic beyond. He had in fact drawn her that way in his 1871 watercolor.

But this southward-facing position would have placed her in an unfriendly attitude, with her back to the city. It also would have meant that passengers on arriving ships would get just a quick frontal view as they came through the Narrows. After that Liberty would seem to turn her back on them as they moved up the harbor.

The sculptor therefore devised an extremely precise new plan. He positioned the Lady so that new arrivals first glimpse her from her right side. Then, as their ship sails on toward the city, they watch her swing gradually into full view. The final view is from her left. To achieve this long-lasting effect, Bartholdi found that he had to have the Statue face in a south-southeasterly direction. Yet the impression most viewers have is that Liberty faces toward the Atlantic and toward Europe.

Attentive observers, viewing the Statue from an incoming vessel, can note a dramatic change in its appearance. At first, viewed from her right, the Lady is seen to be striding vigorously forward. But as the viewer moves to her front, the appearance of movement disappears completely and the Lady seems to be standing quite still, her bearing proud and erect but totally calm.

Bartholdi's careful placement of the Statue also ensured that her handsome profile would be permanently visible from the tip of Manhattan. Brooklynites get the benefit of a full frontal view. Spectators on the west in New Jersey, unfortunately, can see little more than the Lady's back.

At long last, all the problems and questions and frustrations had been resolved. After so many delays and some last-minute postponements, the Lady's gala inauguration was scheduled for October 28, 1886. She was ready for it just in time.

The great day dawned gray, rainy, and blustery. In the words of *Frank Leslie's Illustrated Newspaper,* "The Statue, robed in clouds, towered heavenward in spectral grandeur." The article quickly added that "mere weather cannot dampen American enthusiasm." The city was jammed with an estimated two hundred fifty thousand joyous visitors.

FRANK LESLIE'S ILLUSTRATED NEWSPAPER

VOL. LXIII.] NEW YORK—FOR THE WEEK ENDING OCTOBER 23, 1886.

With only weeks to go before the dedication ceremony on Oct. 28, 1886, workmen raced to finish the interior framework.

Not all were there to celebrate the Statue. The next day's *Times* reported that the police had picked up no fewer than nine pickpockets, all diligently working the happy crowd.

The biggest, most colorful parade New York had ever seen was to proceed down Fifth Avenue and Broadway, with General Stone acting as grand marshal. A naval procession would then sail down the Hudson into the Bay, saluting Liberty as it passed her island.

The reviewing stand for the parade was set up at Madison Square. President Cleveland was there with most of the members of his cabinet. Heading the French delegation was the eighty-two-year-old Ferdinand de Lesseps, builder of the Suez Canal, who had succeeded Laboulaye as head of the French-American Union on the latter's death in 1883. Bartholdi was of course accorded a place of special honor. Members of the French Parliament and government had also come over.

Even the usually stolid *Times* waxed poetic on this occasion. It compared the scene to "a hundred Fourths of July," adding that "it seemed to have rained brass bands during the night. . . ." The crowds lined up to watch the procession were estimated at fully a million persons.

One vivid description of the spectacle was written by José Marti, leader of the Cuban rebels against Spanish rule. He considered Liberty's triumph a good omen for his own people's struggle. "Not an empty spot in the streets," he wrote.

> The twin rivers seem solid land as mist-pearling ships maneuver bow to bow. The Brooklyn Bridge groans under its load of humanity. Sidewalks, portals, balconies, penthouses are covered with a happy throng. . . . Flags fly in hearts, as from buildings. . . .
>
> A song runs all along the route of march. The golden clarion of the Marseillaise flies over the parade. Head bared, the President salutes the tattered banners. As they pass in review, the companies dip their colors and the officers of the French militia raise the hilts of their swords to their lips. . . .

Some twenty thousand persons marched past the applauding dignitaries. Further downtown they passed under a huge triumphal arch erected in front of the *World* building. It bore a huge banner reading, "*Vive L'Entente Fraternelle des Deux Républiques* ['Long Live the Brotherly Friendship of the Two Republics']."

Marti detailed the marchers:

> Regular and Grand Army units, Rochambeau Grenadiers and Italian Rifles, Swiss and Belgian societies, Brooklyn and Philadelphia mounted police, Elks, Masons, students, high-school boys, and the old coach of George Washington bringing up the rear.

The parade over, the president and his entourage boarded the U.S.S. *Dispatch* for the naval review. It comprised over three hundred vessels, including most of the U.S. Atlantic squadron. Adding to the jam in the harbor, according to the *Times,* were

> steamers bearing their thousands; scows plebeian and yachts aristocratic; proud warriors of the sea; ferryboats, freighters, coasting steamers and river craft—everything that could float and more was there. . . .

Pulitzer himself had hired two steamers which carried hundreds of *World* employees and their families out to Bedloe's Island. He and his family rode out on his personal yacht, *Hinda.*

One group was able to enjoy the whole vast spectacle in uncrowded comfort. According to a note in the June 1976 *Alumni Newsletter* of Saint Peter's Preparatory School and College, in Jersey City, "the Padres and students had a grandstand seat for the dedication ceremonies on the roof of the tallest building in the area, the closest school to the Lady with the Lamp."

On the island, a grandstand had been set up for the

two thousand honored guests who would witness the dedication ceremony. Getting the affair started proved more difficult than expected. The uproar around the island was so tremendous that the opening benediction was drowned out by the tooting of ships' whistles.

When he could at last be heard, de Lesseps was the first speaker. He praised America as "the country where individualism is developed in all its powers; [and] where progress is a religion. . . ." He reminded Americans that France had helped "make them powerful and free."

William M. Evarts replied for the American committee with words of appreciation and praise for the liberty-loving French. It had been arranged that when Evarts finished, a young man standing nearby would signal to Bartholdi, waiting impatiently far above in the crown. The sculptor was then to release the rope holding the giant French flag that covered the face of Liberty.

Unfortunately, Evarts chose to pause dramatically at one point in his speech. The youngster misunderstood. He frantically waved his handkerchief at Bartholdi, who promptly and proudly unveiled his Statue.

The din that then broke loose was like nothing ever heard before. Every gun in the harbor, on land and sea, let fly with salvo after salvo. Every ship's captain competed with all the others' shrieking whistles. Every throat cheered itself hoarse. All poor Evarts could do was sit down.

Only when ammunition was starting to run low, and weariness began to take its toll, was it possible to continue.

The next speaker was President Cleveland. Never known as a particularly effective speaker, Cleveland was eloquent on that day. His concluding paragraph is memorable:

> Instead of grasping in her hands the thunderbolts of terror and death, [our Statue] holds aloft the light which illumines the way to man's enfranchisement. We will not forget that Liberty has here made her home; nor shall her chosen altar be neglected. . . . [Her] stream of light shall pierce the darkness of ignorance and man's oppression until Liberty enlightens the world.

The President had earlier issued a proclamation naming the date "Bartholdi Day." He told the sculptor, "You are the greatest man in America today!" It was the proudest moment of Bartholdi's life.

The ceremonies concluded with the reading of a poem written especially for the dedication by the aged American poet, John Greenleaf Whittier. Its pompous style has condemned this work to oblivion. Emma Lazarus's ringing sonnet, which might have aroused profound emotion in that receptive audience, was ignored.

At least two additional ironies marred the occasion. In the first place, many of the wealthy and influential guests invited to attend the ceremonies had stubbornly resisted every appeal to contribute to the pedestal's construction. The general public, which had given so generously of its hard-earned pennies, could only watch from the shore.

Secondly, women were excluded except for Mme. Bartholdi and de Lesseps's granddaughter. The official reason was that women's safety could not be assured in the great crush of people on the island. The women of the New York State Woman Suffrage Association responded by chartering their own boat. It cruised as close to the island as it could get during the ceremonies. The group's leaders could be heard speaking out in praise of the embodiment of Liberty as a woman, and of course in favor of votes for women.

A tremendous fireworks display had been planned for that evening, but the rainy weather forced a postponement. The show had to wait four days. When it was unleashed on November 1, all who beheld it agreed it was a humdinger. Over at Saint Peter's in Jersey City, the faculty and students again cheered from their vantage point on the school roof.

Press reaction to the day's events provided a fascinating study in how perceptions can be shaped by special interests. A few newspapers in the South, which had never been sympathetic to the idea of the Statue, reacted accordingly. The *Augusta* (Georgia) *Chronicle* questioned whether a pagan goddess was really appropriate in a Christian country. The *Mobile* (Alabama) *Register* emphasized that the Statue signified French-American friendship and free government, but nothing beyond that.

To the *New York Irish-American,* the Statue symbolized above all Ireland's continuing struggle against British rule. *L'Echo d'Italia* focused on the number of Italians who had marched in the great parade. The London *Times* reflected resentment over Britain's exclusion from any role in the festivities. It haughtily poked fun at both participants; it was ludicrous for France, which supposedly had too little liberty, to export it to America—which had too much.

Perhaps the most thoughtful reflection appeared in the *New York Herald.* It noted that a big steamship filled with immigrants had passed through the harbor during the ceremonies. The newspaper "wondered what it could have meant to their tired eyes."

That evening, the French delegation was honored at a gala banquet. Nothing very remarkable took place, but there is a charming little sidelight. It seems that the

The view from the torch in the 1880s—an imaginary but accurate rendering, done before the Statue was erected.

officials responsible for arranging the banquet had to defer to the powerful temperance movement, and could not order any wine. Such an oversight would certainly have astonished and might even have outraged the wine-loving French. Count Augustus Gabriel de Vivier Tassin, a French nobleman living in America at that time, had been invited to attend. He was horrified when he learned of this omission. Count Tassin ordered and paid for the wine out of his own pocket.

The members of the French delegation were so delighted when they learned of this kindness that they later arranged to have the count elected to the French Legion of Honor. The much coveted red ribbon which symbolizes this honor is still cherished by his family.

A few weeks later, Pulitzer staged a little ceremony of his own. After sending the committee the *World*'s check for $100,000, he discovered that a little over $1,000 was still left in the pedestal fund. He had commissioned Tiffany's, the famous jewelry firm, to create a trophy for presentation to Bartholdi. The dazzling result was an ornate silver sphere, decorated with a gold and silver world map and a bas-relief of the Statue, and topped by the arm and torch in silver.

An inscription on one side read, "All homage and Thanks to the Great Sculptor, Bartholdi." The other side bore a second inscription: "A Tribute from the New York *World* and over 121,000 Americans to Auguste Bartholdi and the Great Liberty-Loving People of France, 1886."

Bartholdi wrote to the committee on January 30, 1887. He expressed his delight with the "beauty of the pedestal work." His concluding sentence rang with hope and pride: "I have no doubt that with care and looking after, the monument will last as long as those built by the Egyptians."

10
LADY IN THE SPOTLIGHT

The only light that we contribute to the illumination of the world is the light that will shine out of our life as a nation.

— President Woodrow Wilson, after inaugurating a new lighting system for the Statue of Liberty, 1916

In daylight, Liberty looked wonderful. The sunlight traced out and accented every graceful curve of her copper skin. In the low-angled light of early morning and early evening, she almost seemed to be wearing a halo. But if she were to appear equally luminous at night, she would need a lighting system more powerful than any yet devised.

Bartholdi had given this problem a lot of thought. His original plan called for one set of lights in the crown to radiate far and wide. The torch would contain secondary lights.

Then he had a better idea: Powerful lights should be set around the torch. Reflectors on the torch would direct the rays straight upward, producing a vertical shaft of light which, he hoped, would be visible for many miles. A second lighting array was to be placed around the base and pedestal to illuminate the Statue itself. Lights would also be placed in the crown, but these would be for decorative purposes only. They would create the effect of a jeweled diadem.

The electric light, and the power systems to fuel it, had not yet been invented when Bartholdi first made these plans. The light he had in mind would have had to come from kerosene or gas lamps.

Luckily for Bartholdi and his Statue, Edison devised the first working incandescent electric light in 1879. He designed the necessary power plants and power-line systems soon afterward. The technology needed to electrify the Statue had become available just in time.

There was, however, no power plant on Bedloe's Island. And the committee had no funds left for this purpose.

Help came in the form of an offer from Edward H. Goff, president of the American Electric Manufacturing Company. He promised to donate a plant capable of operating twenty lamps of six thousand candlepower each. His firm would also supply and install the necessary lamps, wiring, and appliances. The value of this gift was subsequently estimated at about seven thousand dollars. It was the largest single donation the committee had ever received.

The power plant and lighting system were installed while the Statue was being completed. One major change was made in Bartholdi's plan. It affected the torch. Lieutenant John Millis, an Army electrical expert who had been appointed to supervise the Statue's lighting system, felt that the desired effect would be achieved better if the lights were inside the torch rather than outside. They would create their effect through a circle of glass eighteen inches wide and twenty-five feet long, cut through the torch's copper sheeting.

Millis's official report was confident: "It is predicted that the lights will so illuminate passing clouds that they will be visible for 100 miles or more." The prediction turned out to be much too optimistic.

Soon after sunset on the day the Statue was dedicated, Millis switched the system on. Thousands were watching eagerly from the shore.

From the Battery, only the base of the Statue and the torch could be seen—dimly. At first it was thought that the rainy weather might be at least partly responsible. But when the weather cleared, the effect was not much better.

The *World* commented glumly that the lighted torch looked more like a glowworm than a beacon. Unless some drastic improvements were made, freedom's light would certainly not shine a hundred miles out to sea, or fifty, or even twenty.

Lieutenant Millis wrote to Bartholdi for advice. The sculptor suggested that the Statue be gilded, so that it would reflect light more efficiently. This would probably have helped, but it was far too expensive.

The federal government, having formally accepted the Statue at the dedication ceremony, now placed it in the care of the Lighthouse Board. That agency announced in the spring of 1887 that a new lens, of the type used in lighthouses, would be mounted in the torch. It would be "one of the most powerful fixed lights in the world." But the board acknowledged that the Statue would probably never function as an actual lighthouse.

The new lens, said the board, was "intended more for the purpose of enhancing the grandeur of the statue than as an aid to navigation."

Despite this and other improvements over the next two decades, Liberty's lights remained unimpressive. This was at least partly because the technology needed to support powerful lighting systems was still in a fairly primitive stage of development. More effective lighting for the Statue would have to await further progress in electrical science and engineering.

In 1893 Bartholdi was once again in the United States. He had come to visit the Chicago World's Fair, where several of his new sculptures were on display. But of course he also stopped off in New York to check out the condition of his greatest work.

What he saw disturbed him deeply. He wrote to Major D. P. Heap, chief engineer of the Lighthouse Board, with new suggestions. The lighting problem had gotten worse as the copper skin gradually developed its green patina, which made it darker and less reflective.

If gilding was still considered too expensive, the sculptor wrote, perhaps the Statue could be "painted in such a manner as to make it appear metallic." And if that didn't work, perhaps it would be better not to illuminate the pedestal. Instead, the limited electric power that was available on the island should be conserved "for the light of the torch." A few lights might be "disposed around the pedestal in a decorative way, as a garland. . . ." As for the crown, it might look better "with a central lantern projecting rays alternately tri-colored."

Only the last of these suggestions was ever tried. It looked fine, but it didn't solve the problem. Bigger improvements were needed.

Bartholdi was also concerned about the poor lighting

inside the Statue. Visitors could hardly see well enough to make their way up the stairs, much less see anything around them. Yet the interior, with the intricate workmanship of the pylon and armature and their linkages to the skin, would undoubtedly interest sightseers as they climbed.

He proposed that the interior be illuminated "so as to show the people the arrangement of the work and allow an accurate examination of all the parts." This idea was carried out soon afterward. Ever since, the opportunity to view the interior support system from close up has been one of the most fascinating aspects of a visit to the Statue. Today, with recent additional improvements in the lighting and wider stairways, the experience is even more enjoyable.

One reason why bigger and better lighting improvements were not tried in the 1890s and early 1900s was that Congress was very tight with appropriations. The cost of maintaining the Statue and its lighting system was then over $25,000 a year. Many in Congress were more concerned with reducing these costs than with lighting the Statue.

The Statue lights had to be extinguished for varying periods during these years for lack of funds. In 1902 a bill to appropriate $50,000 for the lighting system was defeated in the House. The lights, it was said, had no practical value as an aid to commerce.

Thus judged useless as a lighthouse, the Statue was transferred from the Lighthouse Board to the War Department, custodian of Bedloe's Island. Except for a small light in her torch, the Lady was virtually invisible at night.

Unfortunately, Bartholdi did not live to see the Statue aglow in the brilliance of modern lighting. The sculptor died at seventy, in 1904, still actively engaged in the campaign to endow his masterwork with a suitable nighttime visual effect. Within a year after his death, his hometown, Colmar, had erected a large bronze statue showing him at work on a small model of the Statue.

Hope for a better lighting system was reborn in 1916, after a series of historic events had brought about changed attitudes. World War I had broken out in 1914. France, along with her allies, was fighting for her life. Then, in 1915, came the sinking of the British ocean liner *Lusitania* by a German submarine. One hundred twenty-eight Americans lost their lives in this disaster. American public opinion was outraged.

Ralph Pulitzer, Joseph's son, was now running the *World*. He felt that the time had come to rescue embattled France's great gift from the darkness. On May 24, 1916, the *World*'s front-page headline read:

STATUE OF LIBERTY TO GLOW
EVERY NIGHT WITH YOUR AID;
WORLD HEADS A NEW FUND

The newspaper pledged to raise $30,000 for a modern lighting system specially designed by General Electric engineers. The only condition was that the government accept the new plant and promise to maintain it.

To start things off, the *World* itself contributed $1,000. It hoped the rest would come in "a fund of pennies and nickels and dimes and dollars," as had the $100,000 raised thirty years before. And just as it had done in the earlier campaign, the paper promised to print the name of every donor no matter how small the donation.

The public reaction was enthusiastic. The mayor of New York, the secretary of war, and the secretary of the navy immediately endorsed the idea. The U.S. Senate unanimously passed a bill accepting the *World*'s offer and guaranteeing maintenance of the new plant. Vice-President Thomas R. Marshall said, "The Statue . . . should always have been lighted up at night. But there is a special reason why it should now be illuminated. It will be prophetic of the coming dawn. . . ." Marshall was referring to the hoped-for victory of the democracies in the war.

To show how the new lights would look—and to stimulate contributions—the Statue was illuminated for about half an hour during the evening of May 31 by eight powerful searchlights of the battleship *Michigan.* A big public meeting had been arranged for that evening in Battery Park, a fine point from which to view the spectacular event. Various groups went out in boats to get an even better look.

Funds began to flow in from all over the country. The Boy Scouts proved persuasive collectors. Equally active was a corps of "Liberty Girls." Movie stars, then a relatively new feature of American life, did their bit to help.

By the Statue's thirtieth anniversary on October 28, the *World* was claiming that some eighty thousand persons had contributed. Oddly, the needed total of $30,000 was not yet in sight. The paper announced that the anniversary would be celebrated in "hundreds of cities" throughout the country as "Liberty Day." Committees had been set up everywhere to organize fund-raising activities.

Installation of the new lighting system was well under way by that time. The lights were scheduled to be switched on in a gala ceremony on December 2. President Wilson had agreed to come for this purpose.

There was an intriguing little mystery connected with

this second fund drive. The *World* never did announce exactly when the $30,000 goal was reached. The secret was not revealed until the Statue's fiftieth anniversary in 1936.

The official souvenir program of the 1936 celebration told the story. It seems that the *World*'s best efforts had not sufficed to raise the entire amount in time for the lighting ceremony. A self-made millionaire named Henry Latham Doherty then came forward to fill the money gap. According to the souvenir program, Doherty

> owned more Lower Manhattan real estate than any other individual. He built a penthouse in Battery Place, where he could see to his heart's content New York harbor and the Statue of Liberty. He thought Liberty too beautiful not to be seen . . . so as a practical patriot he sponsored the illumination, paid the deficit, and never would let the world be told this heretofore unrecorded bit of history.

Doherty's gift "ran into several thousand dollars."

The Statue was now to be illuminated by 246 floodlights, placed at the eleven points of Fort Wood's star shape and on the pedestal balcony. Inside the torch, fifteen electric lamps of five hundred candlepower each were hooked up to a series of flashers, simulating the flickering light of a flame. At the same time a powerful new lighthouse lens replaced the old one, providing a steady bright light to enhance the flame effect.

The new lighting system required more abundant power than could be provided by the little plant on the island. An underwater cable was laid, connecting the Statue's lights with electric-power sources on the mainland.

The torch itself was drastically redesigned. The sculptor selected to do this job, Gutzon Borglum, was already well known for his statues of many famous Americans. His greatest fame would come later, when he carved the gigantic portraits of Washington, Lincoln, Jefferson, and Theodore Roosevelt into the bedrock of Mount Rushmore, South Dakota.

Borglum cut out sections of the sheet copper that formed the "flame" of the torch. He replaced these with about six hundred pieces of tinted cathedral glass, blue at the bottom, amber over most of the surface, red and yellow at the top. The pieces averaged about one foot square. Each was carefully molded to retain the original flamelike shape of Bartholdi's torch.

The new design heightened the torch's visual effect immensely. But it caused problems later. The glass plates were never adequately sealed into place. Whenever it rained, water seeped into the torch and arm, corroding their iron supports.

On the evening of December 2, 1916, President Wilson was in New York harbor aboard the presidential yacht *Mayflower*. When all was ready, he gave the order to fire two signal rockets from the yacht. All ships in the harbor at once turned out their lights. The president then touched a wireless telegraph key, which switched the Statue's new lighting system on. The Lady sprang forth, resplendent in her brilliant new robe of light. The torch beamed her message of hope to the world more intensely than ever before.

At that moment a small plane piloted by a famous woman flyer of that time, Ruth Law, swooped over and around the Statue. She had recently set a new world's record for distance flying by a woman. The next day's *World* reported that Ruth Law had "two streams of white magnesium flame trailing behind her airplane, and the glowing word 'Liberty' shining down from her wings." It was as if she were "flying in a bright rain of fire."

At a banquet at the Waldorf-Astoria Hotel that night, President Wilson expressed the somber thoughts which the otherwise happy occasion had brought to his mind. He had just been reelected to his second term, but his mind was on the imminent danger that the United States would become involved in the war that had been raging in Europe since 1914.

> The only light that we contribute to the illumination of the world is the light that will shine out of our life as a nation. . . . Throughout the last two years there has come more and more into my heart the conviction that peace is going to come to the world only with Liberty.

Four months later, Wilson regretfully asked Congress for a declaration of war against Germany and her allies. Our war aim, he said, was "to make the world safe for democracy."

Soon the Lady was lighting the way for ships crowded with American soldiers, on their way to battle on the western front. A quarter of a century later, she would have to perform this grim duty all over again.

For nearly a decade after the new lighting system was installed, the lights were on every evening from seven to eleven P.M. In 1925 an automatic system was installed, with a clock control. From that year until the mid-1950s, the Statue was occasionally illuminated from sunset to sunrise. It all depended on how much money Congress was willing to provide.

Increasingly frequent complaints began to be heard that the lights were casting ugly shadows over some parts of Liberty's face. A major overhaul was decided on. Still more powerful lamps replaced those of 1916 in the fort's eleven salients, on the pedestal, and in the torch. A blinker system went into the crown. The light given off by the new system totaled a whopping five hundred thousand candlepower.

But more interesting than the new lights is the story of how they were turned on. The occasion was the eve of the Statue's forty-fifth anniversary, October 27, 1931. Chosen to light the new system was Mlle. Josie Laval, the young daughter of French Premier Pierre Laval. The ceremony was broadcast over the NBC radio network.

Mlle. Laval was in a specially equipped room on the 102nd floor of the then brand-new Empire State Building. When the signal was given, she passed her hand over a Knowles tube, an extremely sensitive silver glass globe. It transmitted a radio signal to a plane circling over the Statue. The pilot released a magnesium flare, triggering a photoelectric cell on the Statue which turned on the new lights.

The event later produced an unexpected irony. The father of the young lady who had so gaily rekindled Liberty's light was executed as a traitor to his country after World War II. Pierre Laval, once again serving as premier during the war, had collaborated with the Nazis occupying France. He had been no friend to liberty.

America's entry into World War II in 1941 produced new problems. The German air force's devastating blitz against London and the other cities of England had shown what bomber aircraft massed into great fleets could do. Though the likelihood of such attacks on American cities seemed remote, the possibility could not be ignored.

The Lady's lights were extinguished once again. As the *Times* pointed out, the illuminated Statue "would be a pretty good guide for bombers headed for Manhattan." Only two 200-watt lamps were left glowing in the torch "for the benefit of our own airplane pilots." The Statue remained open to visitors, however.

The threat of bombing, which turned out not to be very real, was not the only reason for turning out the lights. It was a kind of national sacrifice. It was a pledge that the nation would return to its normal ways only when Hitler and the other brutal aggressors who were then darkening the world were defeated.

On New Year's Eve, 1943, Liberty's lights flashed three dots and a dash. This is Morse code for the letter *V*, which had become the Allies' symbol for victory over the aggressors.

The lights flashed *V* again on D-Day, June 6, 1944, heralding one of the great turning points of the war. That was the day when American, British, and Canadian forces stormed ashore on the coast of Normandy, in Nazi-occupied France, launching the campaign that culminated in the collapse of Nazi Germany.

The war did not prevent further lighting improvements. By the end of 1944, a new system had been installed that was so brilliant it was said to give twenty-five hundred times the brightness of full moonlight.

The new system was switched on permanently on V-E Day (Victory in Europe Day), May 8, 1945, to celebrate the Nazis' surrender. The sudden brilliance gave the entire nation's spirits a badly needed lift after the long years of the wartime dimout, when all the big seaport cities had to keep their lights low. But of all who rejoiced at the Lady's rekindled splendor, none can have been more deeply moved than the battle-weary GIs returning home.

April 4, 1957, was not a very special date on the calendar. But it became very special for Lady Liberty. Up to that time she had only been lit for a few hours every evening. On that date, dusk-to-dawn illumination was at last started as a regular and permanent feature. It has continued ever since.

By the mid-1970s, America was preparing for the biggest party in years: the celebration of its bicentennial, the two-hundredth anniversary of the nation's independence. Lady Liberty, symbol of the shared French–American struggle that had made independence a reality, would obviously play a central role in the festivities. But to do it properly she needed still another, more powerful set of lights. A new system was designed to provide four times the illumination of the existing one.

Work on it had to be rushed, so that it would be ready for the Fourth of July, 1976, the date selected for Operation Sail. Hundreds of graceful sailing ships from all over the world were scheduled to parade through New York harbor and circle Liberty Island (The name was changed from Bedloe's Island by act of Congress in 1956).

Liberty responded with new golden lights in her torch. Her handsome head gleamed in the rays of thirteen new floodlights so big that each weighed two and a half tons.

Ten years ahead lay yet another big day. October 28, 1986, would mark the Lady's own hundredth birthday. Planning got under way in the early 1980s for a top-to-bottom cleanup and overhaul that would restore her to prime condition for at least another century. Every available resource in the nation was mobilized in a tremendous new effort to raise funds. Both the Statue and nearby Ellis Island, the former immigrant reception center, were to benefit.

The Statue's lighting, both interior and exterior, was scheduled for still another updating. The torch was the biggest problem. Its upper half, with the flame, had long been leaky in bad weather. Corrosion had progressed so far inside and outside the torch that it was beyond repair. It would have to be replaced.

On the Fourth of July, 1984, the top half of the battered old torch was gently detached from the rest. In the words of the construction manager, it was lovingly lowered to the ground "like a baby, a 100-year-old baby." A special showplace for it was prepared in the museum at the Statue's base.

The replacement torch is an embodiment of Bartholdi's original plan in many ways. It is solid copper, as he had thought it should be, with no cutout panels (of glass or any other material). The copper was hammered by hand, by French craftsmen specially imported for the task. First a plaster mold was made from the old flame. Then a wood mold was made from that. Finally, copper sheeting was placed inside and hammered into shape against the wood, creating a precise duplicate of the original. Even Bartholdi's advice about gilding the torch to make it a better reflector was carried out. It was plated first with nickel, and then with gold by an electrically charged brush. Powerful new floodlights focus directly on it. The result is a luminous golden glow reflected higher and farther than ever before. It is a light that truly seems capable of enlightening the world.

· 11 ·
ADVENTURES OF THE LADY

My idea has always been that [the island] would be in the future, a kind of Pantheon for the glories of American independence . . . . This island should become a sort of pilgrimage. . . .
— Bartholdi, in a letter to a friend, 1890

A lot can happen to a lady in a hundred years—and it has, to this Lady.

She has received homage from every U.S. president of the past hundred years. High-ranking foreign dignitaries have come from afar to pay her tribute. She has played her part in patriotic ceremonies, and has had a part forced upon her in anti-American demonstrations.

Hurricane winds, swirling blizzards, cloudbursts of rain, blazing suns have attacked her. Lightning once hit her electric power station and blacked her out for a few hours.

Born at a time when New York harbor teemed with trim sailing ships, the Lady has witnessed their replacement by giant ocean liners and thundering jumbo jets.

For the first forty-four years of her existence she could observe the always fiercely contested America's Cup yacht races. That famous annual international competition was held close-by until it was moved to the less-crowded waters of Newport, Rhode Island, in 1930.

The Statue has welcomed a million immigrants a year to America, then seen immigration slow to a trickle, then seen it revive.

The number of visiting tourists has risen steadily since her unveiling. Today she accommodates nearly two million every year. She has had to suffer the bizarre antics of some of these visitors. Every inch of her interior that could be reached has been defaced with grafitti, to be cleaned up and repainted and besmirched again.

The Statue of Liberty reservation originally extended only to the two acres of Fort Wood, while the rest of the island was under military control. Today the Statue of Liberty National Monument includes all fifteen acres of Liberty Island. Once it was governed by the Lighthouse Board, then by the Department of War, and since 1933 by the National Park Service of the Department of the Interior. Its extensive staff includes the uniformed Park Rangers, who act as visitors' guides; security, maintenance, and clerical personnel; librarians and archivists. Heading the administration of the national monument is the superintendent.

The Lady did not, could not, go through an entire century without damage. A part here, a part there, has had to undergo repair or even replacement. As we have seen, her lighting system in particular has been revitalized many times. But through it all she has remained herself: unique, instantly recognized, universally revered.

She has also been a magnet, attracting an incredible

assortment of individuals both invited and uninvited.

The first time visitors were startled by an unexpected spectacle at the Statue was in 1892. They beheld a man who seemed to be dangling from a rope fastened to the torch, and who kept swinging from one point on the Statue's skin to another. Actually he was a professional steeplejack, and he had been hired to search the surface for leaks. According to the *Times,* the nimble fellow got around out there "as would a fly." But the winds buffeted him roughly, and he had to quit after finding nearly fifty leaks.

Much grimmer was an event that shocked visitors in 1929. As they watched in helpless amazement, a despondent man climbed out of a window in the crown. Before anyone could stop him the man jumped, glanced off the Lady's breast, and plunged to his death at her feet.

The only other death that has ever occurred on the island came in the late 1970s. A woman suffered a fatal heart attack while climbing the long stairway to the crown.

Happily, the island has also witnessed two births. One of the Statue's lighting technicians was presented with a son in 1899. Another employee's baby boy was born there in 1918. Both families were housed on the island. Today, the Statue's superintendent, his family, and certain other employees of the National Park Service make their homes within its bounds. The rest of the staff rides the ferry to and from the island each day.

There have been adventures that endangered the Statue's very existence. In 1911, twenty-five tons of dynamite exploded while being unloaded at a Jersey City pier, just across the harbor to the west. The immediate area was devastated, but the Statue suffered only a few broken windows and shattered light bulbs in the torch. Eiffel's interior framework proved its value as the Statue withstood the shock with no structural damage.

That mishap turned out to be only a preview of a far worse disaster five years later. With World War I under way in Europe, the Jersey City piers had become a major shipping point for munitions. At Black Tom Island (actually a peninsula jutting out from the Jersey shore toward the Statue), there were numerous freight cars and barges loaded with explosives on any given day. A nitroglycerine plant had been built close-by.

On July 29, 1916, a fire of mysterious origin broke out. German saboteurs, determined to prevent American-made arms from reaching their country's enemies, were almost certainly responsible.

The ensuing series of explosions caused near-total destruction and many deaths in the Black Tom area. Windows were blown out in downtown Manhattan. Fragments of shell came crashing down as far away as Governors Island. Some of them bombarded the Statue. Doors and windows were blown off houses on Bedloe's Island. Shock waves from the explosion tore about a hundred iron bolts inside the Statue from their sockets. Whizzing steel splinters chipped the skin and pedestal. Most serious of all, the torch-bearing arm was badly shaken. Soon afterward, it was closed to the public.

On the lighter side, there have been several occasions when heedless visitors have been stranded on Bedloe's Island after visiting hours. In 1904, two young women were locked into the Statue for much of the night. They had stayed up in the observation chamber in the crown, admiring the view, till after sunset. When they came down, the door was locked. Hours later a soldier on sentry duty heard the captives calling from a window in the pedestal, and he released them. The island's army detachment not only fed and cared for the frightened women but even called out the garrison band to cheer them up.

In 1936, a pair of young lovers had found some small measure of privacy on the terrace atop the pedestal, behind the Statue. When the National Park Rangers made their final tour of the day before leaving, they somehow failed to spot the couple. All doors were, of course, locked. Not until late in the evening did a sergeant of the Military Police detachment hear the couple's cries for help. Having no keys to the Statue, he had to get fire ladders to reach them.

Like other much-publicized monuments, the Statue has also attracted its share of crazies. On a rather cool day in 1945 the superintendent was notified that someone was swimming off the west shore of the island. He found a twenty-six-year-old blonde woman, dressed in a herringbone suit and a camel's hair coat, splashing about in shallow water. The superintendent called to her, but she giggled and waved to him and went right on having a fine time. He finally had to wade in and pull her out. The woman, entirely cheerful but chilled and damp, was taken to a psychiatric ward in a New York City hospital that evening.

In the late 1970s a man ascended to the crown and announced that agents of President Carter were poisoning him. He wrapped himself in an American flag, lay down, and prepared to die. Rangers removed him as gently as they could and sent him for psychiatric treatment.

A few years later a homeless twenty-one-year-old man smashed an observation window in the crown, climbed out onto the Statue's head, and showered the astonished tourists below with leaflets. He proclaimed himself a write-in candidate for mayor of New York. The only way he could be approached safely was by lowering a police officer from the torch. Two hours of skilled persuasion were still required to calm the deranged individual, before he was captured and literally brought down to earth.

Even more weird was the adventure that befell the Lady in June 1983. A young couple had flown two ultra-light airplanes across the country. For some utterly incomprehensible reason, they decided it would be fun to make their landing on Liberty Island. The male pilot did manage to put his tiny plane down safely in the extremely limited space at the base of the Statue.

His female companion looked as if she were going to overshoot the chosen spot and land in the water. Trying to stop her plane, he grabbed a wing. The plane swung around, hit him in the face, and caromed into the wall of the base. By sheer good fortune, neither pilot was badly hurt. They had more trouble explaining their lunatic choice of a landing field than recovering from their injuries.

The first political demonstration to be staged at the Statue was the one carried out by woman-suffrage advocates during the dedication ceremony in 1886. A second, decidedly different one, took place forty years later. Its sponsor was an organization known as the World War Veterans Light Wines and Beer League.

Three league members arrived at the Statue with bulky parcels. They told the guards they had just arrived in town and were still carrying their personal effects.

When they got to the crown, they opened the parcels and draped two sixty-foot black-crepe streamers from the windows. This was their way of "mourning" what they regarded as a grievous loss of liberty. The purpose of their demonstration was to win popular support for the repeal of Prohibition, the ban on the sale and manufacture of alcoholic beverages enacted in 1920.

It was no accident that the leader and spokesman for these demonstrators was a public-relations expert. He had chosen the cleverest possible location to stage his group's action. Almost anything unusual happening around the Statue is virtually guaranteed plenty of publicity. These demonstrators probably did not realize that they were setting an example that would have all too many publicity-seeking imitators in the years to come.

Political demonstrations at the Statue began in earnest in the mid-1950s. They have erupted periodically ever since. An anticommunist Hungarian patriot carried out one of the earliest in 1956. He was protesting the Soviet Union's brutal repression of a recent uprising by his countrymen. He climbed to the crown, broke open the locked door leading to the torch, and unfurled a Hungarian and an American flag from the torch balcony. Afterward he said, "We want the same liberty in Hungary as in the U.S."

Pro-Castro Cuban rebels followed his example the following year. But after Castro took power in 1960, it was the anti-Castro refugees who repeatedly occupied the Statue in protest against his regime.

Fortunately for the Statue, in 1965 there was one demonstration that did *not* happen. A small group of extremists, calling themselves the Black Liberation Front, plotted to blow up the Statue, the Washington Monument, and the Liberty Bell in Philadelphia. They were assisted by a young Canadian woman, who smuggled a considerable quantity of dynamite from Montreal into the United States.

The plot was revealed by an undercover police officer, and the plotters were arrested. Their leader told the police they had chosen this means to dramatize the plight of blacks in America. Their intention was to plant the dynamite at the point where the Lady's upraised arm is linked to her shoulder. The charge would have been sufficient to blow off both the arm and the head.

The Canadian woman turned government witness and testified against the others. The leader and two of his followers received prison sentences. David L. Moffitt, superintendent of the Statue, expressed the perplexity felt by many: "I can understand demonstrations of all kinds. But why would they want to destroy freedom?"

With the rise of the women's-rights movement in the 1960s and 1970s, it was inevitable that the Lady would be enlisted. Activists staged a major demonstration on Liberty Island in 1972, taking over the Statue for a brief time. They hung a banner from the windows in the crown which read, "Women of the World, Unite."

Included among the propaganda materials that they distributed were picture-postcard-size photos, in which the Lady's uplifted right hand no longer held the torch. Instead the hand was depicted as a clenched fist, symbol of revolt. The photos gained interest from the fact that they had been signed by Beatles star John Lennon and his wife, Yoko Ono. The women's rights movement was just one of the causes to which this celebrated couple lent its support.

A new cause brought on a new group of demonstrators in 1971. By that time, the United States had been heavily engaged in the Vietnam conflict for nearly a decade.

Public opinion was badly divided as to whether we should persist or abandon the struggle, which seemed to be getting nowhere.

On December 27, 1971, fifteen Vietnam veterans who opposed the war seized control of the Statue. They vowed to stay until New Year's Eve. The ex-soldiers had planned their operation in military style, down to the last detail. They brought their own food, a bag full of coins for the pay phones, and even plastic bags in which to collect their garbage. They used the phones to notify the media and, presumably, to contact their friends and families.

At five P.M., when the last tourists left, they hid in the basement. Later, when the night watchman came in on his rounds, they persuaded him to spread the word that they would not cause any destruction or violence. Though well trained and experienced in the use of weapons, the veterans were not armed.

That night, they flew an American flag upside down from the crown, the traditional distress signal. They subsequently moved the flag up to the torch.

No attempt was made to evict them or use force against them. The authorities did, however, obtain a court order directing the demonstrators to leave or face imprisonment. After a day and a half, feeling that they had made their point, the veterans quietly departed. They had neither damaged the Statue nor left behind any trash. There were no arrests.

During the late 1970s and early 1980s the Lady became the unwilling hostess to a whole series of demonstrations stemming from political struggles in areas as far apart as Iran and Puerto Rico. But the most dismaying protest was the one staged in 1980 by two Americans.

The veterans depart after their nonviolent demonstration, December 28, 1971.

They arrived on the island with mountain-climbing equipment concealed in duffel bags. Somehow they eluded the guards, and at about ten A.M. the pair proceeded to climb the outside of the Statue. The two men were out of reach by the time they were discovered.

When one of them had reached the small of the Lady's back, and the other was poised behind her right knee, they unfurled a twenty-five-foot banner protesting the alleged frame-up and long-term imprisonment of a California black radical convicted of murder. They stayed at their chosen posts all night despite the bitter cold, and came down the next morning.

At first their climbing apparatus was believed to have done extensive damage to the delicate copper skin. It turned out that they had relied mainly on suction cups to aid their ascent. Like the Vietnam veterans, these men too had been concerned about the Lady's well-being. They had inflicted no serious harm. Arrested on the spot, they suffered minor penalties along with a stern warning against any repetition.

Though they never did try again, they had their imitators four years later. It happened on August 6, 1984, anniversary of the atomic bombing of Hiroshima. At that time the Statue was surrounded by aluminum scaffolding, as work progressed on the major renovation that had been planned prior to its hundredth anniversary.

Four members of a nuclear-disarmament group called Greenpeace climbed partway up the scaffolding and, in the by-then traditional manner, unfurled a big banner. It read "Give Me Liberty from Nuclear Weapons—Stop Testing." After five hours they came down, were arrested and charged with criminal trespass.

In the one case in which a serious effort to inflict damage was actually carried out, the breakage was negligible. A small bomb exploded in an exhibition room in the Statue's base in June 1980. Luckily, the explosion occurred in the evening and no tourists were present. The room contained historical materials about the Statue, including the bronze plaque inscribed with Emma Lazarus's sonnet. The Statue had to be closed for just one day for the cleanup.

This explosion occurred at a time when terrorism was rising to new heights throughout the world. Several terrorist groups, eager to claim credit for it, phoned the newspapers and TV stations: anti-Castro Cubans, American Nazis, Puerto Rican nationalists, the Palestine Liberation Movement. But the authorities finally concluded that the most probable perpetrators were Croatian freedom fighters opposed to the communist regime in Yugoslavia. Remarkably, even these desperate characters were apparently unwilling to risk the storm of public outrage that would have ensued if they had caused Liberty any major damage.

Soon afterward, Liberty Island's resident population of twelve persons received a welcome addition in the shape of a new mascot. She was a handsome golden retriever named Talli, and she was specially trained to sniff out explosives.

Not all the Lady's adventures have been so grim. She has hostessed many proud and happy occasions too. One of these came along in 1936, the year of the Statue's Golden Jubilee. President Franklin D. Roosevelt came out to the island to deliver the fiftieth-anniversary address. He restated the nation's gratitude for the resplendent gift from "our old neighbor and friend across the sea." Of the immigrants who had responded to the Statue's beckoning light he said: "They brought to us strength and moral fiber developed in a civilization centuries old, but fired anew by the dream of a better life in America." This country had become "the place of the second chance" for people all over the world.

Interestingly, one of the speakers at the banquet held that evening was André de Laboulaye, grandson of the man who had conceived the idea of the Statue. M. de Laboulaye was now France's ambassador to the United States.

In the 1950s, a group of citizens formed a committee to create a museum commemorating the immigrants' contributions to American life. It was to be built into the base of the Statue. The committee sponsored a symbolic ceremony on June 25, 1955. Pinches of earth from all the states and territories of the U.S. and thirty-four foreign countries were mixed in a bowl, taken up into the torch, and scattered over the island. Some of the mixed soil was saved. It was deposited in the museum's cornerstone, which was laid on the Statue's seventy-fifth anniversary in 1961.

The American Museum of Immigration was opened to the public in 1972. Its two-tiered granite structure contains a rich array of permanent and changing exhibits. Today's visitors can divide their time between their tour of the Statue, a look at the other statuary on the grounds, and an exploration of the museum.

The year 1965 brought an auspicious visit by President Lyndon Johnson. As senator, vice-president, and now as president, he had been struggling for years to liberalize the nation's immigration laws. These had been tightened drastically in 1924 and again in the 1950s. Now, with his long-sought new law at last enacted by Congress, the president chose to sign the measure with a dramatic flourish at the base of the Statue, facing Ellis Island.

The question of which state should have jurisdiction over Liberty Island recently became an issue between New York and New Jersey. The island is geographically located inside the borders of New Jersey, but an 1833 agreement between the two states assigned legal jurisdiction over both Liberty Island and Ellis Island to New York. The agreement carries the formal approval of the United States Congress, as all interstate compacts are required to do.

A not entirely serious symptom of the dispute was a recent proposal by a New Jersey legislator that the Lady be mounted on a swivel. She could then be rotated slowly so that New Jerseyans, who now see only the Lady's back from their shores, could share more attractive views with their neighbors. The ingenious idea seems unlikely to be adopted.

Late in 1984, however, New Jersey authorities filed suit in federal court to have the two islands returned to the control of their state. The case may be long and drawn-out. New York will resist the change with every means at its disposal.

Liberty's finest moment till now came in 1976, America's bicentennial. The celebrations surrounding this historic milestone made it the most spectacular Fourth of July ever. The starring role was, naturally, reserved for the Lady.

The eve of the Fourth saw her lit up by a tremendous fireworks display that seemed to keep topping one dazzling effect with another even more astounding. Adding to the din were the salvoes of hundreds of guns ashore and afloat, which fired more than three thousand shells.

"Operation Sail," celebrating America's 200th birthday, July 4, 1976.

The spectators' cheers and applause rose to a roar when a helicopter appeared, towing a 60-by-100-foot flag outlined in red, white, and blue lights.

Following instructions which had been broadcast and published in the newspapers earlier, many spectators were carrying radios. As the festivities came to their climax, the public was instructed to face the Statue and,

accompanied by a band heard over the air, to join in singing "The Star-Spangled Banner." Never can the anthem have been voiced with keener enthusiasm.

For the Fourth itself, the planners came up with a new idea well suited to a celebration centered around New York harbor. It was called Operation Sail. A magnificent array of tall sailing ships was assembled from all over the world. There were two hundred twenty-five of them, under the flags of thirty-one countries. As hundreds of thousands scrambled for good vantage points on the surrounding shorelines, and millions more watched on television, the sleek ships came gliding on the wind through the harbor. With every inch of dazzling sunlit canvas stretched and snapping in the breeze, they wheeled in stately procession and circled Liberty Island.

The tall ships were followed by a majestic international naval review. Some fifty warships from twenty-two countries took their turn at saluting Liberty. Through it all, the harbor waters were covered, in the words of the *Times,* by "a virtually unbroken bridge of small craft that reached from the shores of Brooklyn to the coast of New Jersey."

The Lady had witnessed many gala moments, but Operation Sail was far and away the most gracious tribute she—and her adopted country—had ever received. It was hardly over before planning began on an even grander rally of the tall ships for the Statue's own centennial in 1986.

One thing that has *not* happened to the Statue and its island is the literal fulfullment of its creator's dream. In 1890 Bartholdi expounded his vision to a friend:

> My idea has always been that [the island] would be in the future, a kind of Pantheon for the glories of American independence. That you would build around the monument of Liberty the statues of your very great men, and collect there all the noble memories. This island should become a sort of pilgrimage. . . .

Only the last of these hopes has become a reality.

Every day of the year, in every kind of weather, Americans and other visitors crowd in on their pilgrimage to the world's most famous Lady.

But Liberty does have other kinds of company on her island. Two groups of statues have been set in place. They are not the kind Bartholdi imagined.

One group stands in the lobby at the base of the Statue. It consists of eight large bronzes illustrating the immigrant experience. Through symbolic portraits of immigrants of various ages based on historic photographs, the sculptures capture the emotional impact of the newcomers' hopeful but often agonizing journey between the two worlds.

The other group graces a sculpture garden at the western end of the island. It portrays the five individuals most closely associated with the Statue: Bartholdi, Laboulaye, Eiffel, Lazarus, and Pulitzer. Bartholdi is shown working on a small model of the Statue. His friend and mentor Laboulaye, the scholar, appears deep in thought. Eiffel studies a miniature of his famous tower. Emma Lazarus holds a book, her face wearing the pensive expression befitting a poet in the throes of creation. Pulitzer, appropriately, scans the front page of a newspaper.

The justly acclaimed creator of both groups is Phillip Ratner of Maryland. Other sculptures by Ratner can be seen at several leading museums. His works for the Statue exhibits were financed by private donors and given to the National Park Service in the early 1980s. Ratner has also sculpted a group of thirty-five additional pieces on the immigration theme, which have been exhibited in major cities throughout the country. They will eventually be placed on permanent exhibition on

Bartholdi at work on a model of the Statue, part of Philip Ratner's group of sculptures on Liberty Island.

Ellis Island—where Ratner's own grandparents arrived around the turn of the century.

Bartholdi envisioned a rather different set of sculptures surrounding his masterpiece. Nevertheless, it seems likely he would be pleased with the Lady's new companions.

12
THE LADY GETS A TOTAL CHECKUP

You gotta be extra careful working on the Statue. . . . I try to do the best I can and make sure we do it right. I hope I don't make a boo-boo.

— Angelo Bommarido, construction crew foreman, 1984

Lady Liberty got the most thorough physical exam of her life in the early 1980s. Her centennial celebration was then in the planning stages. She had to look right for it. More importantly, she had to *be* right for it.

A team of French and American architects and engineers spent two years going over her from torch to toe. They tested her every way modern science and technology could devise. Vibration gauges and strain gauges, wind meters, air-quality monitors, computer-generated graphics were all brought into play. Experts analyzed the Statue's whole geometry, with special focus on its stress points.

Researchers tried hard to find the original drawings and diagrams worked out by the Statue's creators. These might have supplied helpful insights; but an exhaustive research effort turned up only ten pages of Eiffel's original calculations. One of the American architects described these as "intriguing, interesting, but not conclusive."

When all the testing had been completed, the Lady failed the exam. Her interior support structures were found to be corroding and weakening. Her exterior good looks were deteriorating. The experts explored, calculated, consulted, and finally presented the National Park Service with an elaborate plan for repairs and refurbishments.

The job would be expensive. The experts' first cost estimates ranged between \$20 million and \$30 million. Later judgments raised the amount toward the \$40 million mark (contrast this with the entire original cost for building the Statue: only \$250,000!). The project would start in January 1984, and would take at least two years.

The first step was to cage the entire Statue in three hundred tons of aluminum scaffolding, the largest such free-standing structure ever built. The scaffolding would give workmen access to every part of the Statue's exterior, and support the wire-mesh elevator designed to haul them and their tools up and down the famous facade. The Statue was to be kept open to visitors as much as possible while the work went forward. Even when the interior had to be closed off, the island and the museum would still receive visitors.

Work had to be finished in time for the first of the Statue's centennial celebrations, scheduled for the Fourth of July, 1986. A second gala was planned for the hundredth anniversary of the unveiling on October 28. The president would then rededicate the Statue for its second century.

Liberty temporarily in a cage, 1984.

This was not the Lady's first touch-up. She got a light going-over when she was just twenty-one years old, in 1907. Workmen laid new granite facings inside and outside the pedestal. The interior framework got a new paint job. Most importantly for her visitors, the first elevator was installed. It carried sightseers from the base to the top of the pedestal, where they could start their 171-step twelve-story climb up the spiral stairway leading to the crown.

War department engineers made a special study of the skin at that time. They were concerned about the green patina that had gradually spread over it, as a result of the interaction between the copper and the atmosphere. Was the patina harming the skin in any way? Should it be removed, so that the original copper would once more be visible? The engineers' conclusion was that the patina "softened the outlines of the Statue and made it beautiful." Far from doing harm, it helped protect the skin.

It wasn't until thirty years later that the Lady got her second thorough examination. It showed up problems so serious that she had to be closed to visitors for twenty months, from April 1937 to December 1938. The repairs cost $1,700,000.

The most spectacular repair involved the seven rays radiating from the crown. The copper rays themselves were still in fine shape, but the steel supports inside them were dangerously corroded. Visitors to the island could watch from below as workmen clambered precariously around the head, removing the rays one at a time, inserting new rust-resistant supports, and replacing the rays.

The stairway inside the Lady's upper body was also in poor condition. It was rebuilt. Then the whole interior was repainted, including an application of rust-retarding red lead to the iron framework.

In bad weather, storm water pouring off the Statue tended to seep into the pedestal. Workmen put in what the *Times* called "a 250-foot copper apron to keep Miss Liberty's feet dry." The apron consisted of copper sheathing around the bottom of the Statue.

By 1946, the Lady's insides were so badly defaced by sixty years of graffiti, piled up in layer upon layer, that something had to be done. Most of the ugly markings had been made with lipstick. The remedy was to paint all seventy thousand square feet of the interior with a new plastic compound specially created to keep lipstick on the surface, preventing it from eating through the paint and into the metal underneath. It could then be washed off with relative ease.

Then came the checkup of the early 1980s. It revealed a whole range of ailments starting right at the top.

Air pollution, acid rain, high winds, and every kind of weather had done their worst to the torch. It was so badly corroded that small chunks had actually begun to drop off. The possibility that larger pieces would endanger people below was real. Almost the entire torch, from the level of its little balcony to the tip of its "flame," would have to be replaced. The new torch would be of gilded solid copper, and would reflect powerful new lights beamed at it from the outside.

The examination also revealed that the forty-two-foot, twenty-ton upraised right arm had been improperly connected to the central structure from the start. This incorrect linkage had made the shoulder joint weak, and it was getting weaker. The arm swayed ever more alarmingly when the winds blew. There was a definite risk of structural failure.

STATUE OF LIBERTY RESTORATION

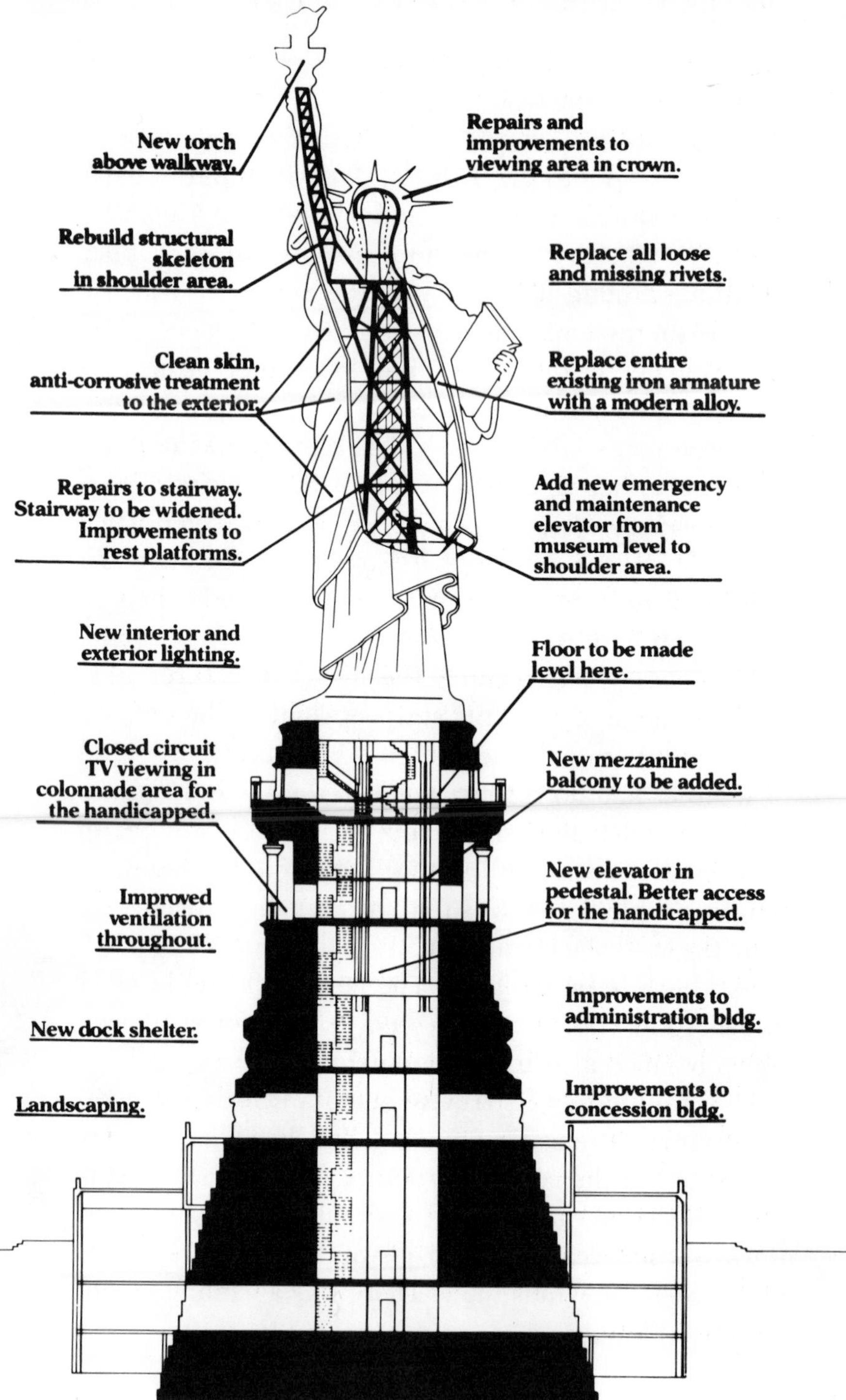

The "torch-to-toes" treatment of the mid-1980s.

At first it was thought that the arm would have to removed, so that it could be repaired on the ground. Ultimately it was decided that the scaffolding could be built strong enough to support the arm while it was being worked on.

Also discovered during this inspection was the fact that the head too had been set inaccurately when the Statue was erected back in 1886. The head was an astonishing two feet off center. The misalignment placed unnecessary stress on the inner framework, but structural analysis showed this was not serious enough to cause concern. One of the architects was asked whether the repair teams would attempt to rearrange the Lady's head. "She looks beautiful the way she is," he told the reporters. "We do not intend to deal with her cosmetically."

The head's displacement had caused another, wholly unexpected problem. One of the rays extending out of the crown had been rubbing against the arm for years, and had worn a hole in it. The planned adjustments in the arm's connections to the body would shift the arm just enough to eliminate this difficulty.

As for the three hundred copper plates that make up the skin, they got an inch-by-inch scrutiny. Specialists did an "elemental scan" of tiny skin samples. They used X-ray fluorescence to determine the precise extent of erosion, damage, and deterioration.

The results showed that the copper plates had come through their hundred years of buffeting by New York's turbulent climate in surprisingly good shape. Erosion and air pollution had thinned all the plates down, but only two percent of them were in really critical condition. Years of weathering had distorted some plates out of their original shape, and others were discolored. New plates would have to be molded and substituted for these. Every hole, chink, and chip in the skin would be sealed.

Then a powerful steam spray, using a mild detergent, would remove the grime of the years. The Lady had enjoyed only three baths before this, in 1916, 1927, and 1932. Special care would be taken to ensure that the cleaning removed none of the skin's beautiful and protective green patina.

But what could be done about the new copper plates that replaced those worn beyond repair? Unless they got some sort of special treatment, they would make parts of the Statue look like a new penny. They could be given an artificial patina with acid solutions, but that might cause stuctural weak points.

The problem was solved by making a highly unusual deal with the Bell Laboratories. The Bell Telephone Company, which uses vast quantities of copper wiring in its communications and electronic equipment, was interested in studying the long-term effects of corrosion on copper. The corroded portions of the Statue's skin were a perfect subject for this purpose. In exchange for the opportunity to examine these under electron microscopes, Bell Labs donated a large copper roof from one of its older buildings. The roof had developed a green patina over the years that closely matched that of the Statue. It would be cut up and used for the patching job.

Of the three hundred thousand rivets that hold the skin to the strapwork inside, about twenty-five thousand had either popped out or been damaged badly enough to need replacement. That sounds like a lot; another way of looking at it is to consider that an impressive ninety-two percent of the original rivets were still doing their job.

The empty rivet holes and other tiny openings in the skin had allowed moisture to enter the interior. Pockets of condensation had formed, causing corrosion in the armature.

The worst problem affected the two thousand iron bars of the strapwork. The two-inch-thick bars stretched over a total area of more than two miles inside of the skin. Some were so badly rusted that they were only half their original thickness. Many of the iron saddles clamping the strapwork bars to the skin had worked loose. No major repairs or replacements had been carried out on this essential part of the armature since 1886.

The prescribed remedy was drastic: replace all of the iron strapwork and saddles with bars made of a modern metal alloy, an industrial form of stainless steel. This material was not only rustproof; it had also been treated with electricity to add strength.

The detailed plan for the Statue's renovation included thoughtful consideration of its visitors' comfort and enjoyment—and of their complaints. The visitors' most common complaint, next to the rigors of the climb to the crown, centered on the quality of the air they had to breathe while making the ascent. In summer it was sometimes so stiflingly hot and humid that the authorities had to post a warning notice at the entrance. In winter it was cold and dank. Tests showed that when there were large crowds, the levels of carbon dioxide were high.

The new plan provides for a vastly improved ventilation system throughout the structure. Air-conditioning and heating systems were considered and then rejected. The Statue's thin (three thirty-seconds of an inch) skin would have dissipated any cooling or heating effect almost as fast as these could be produced. The new system is designed to draw fresh air in and circulate it efficiently.

Visitors of the future would have a more pleasant time getting up to the viewing chamber in the crown. An air-conditioned, double-decker, hydraulic, glass-enclosed elevator would replace the nearly seventy-year-old enclosed model that had once carried people to the top of the pedestal.

The transparent walls of the new elevator would enable visitors to enjoy sweeping new views of the interior of the base and pedestal. These had originally been designed to give a powerful impression of colossal open spaces, but over the years a number of concrete platforms had been built which obstructed the view. All such nonessential structures would be removed.

As tourists emerged from the elevator at the top of the pedestal, they would no longer have to deal with the awkward thirty-inch width of the original double-spiral stairway. The plans called for widening the stairway, improving the little rest areas all along the way, and removing the wire-mesh screens that formerly enclosed the stairway. Visitors would now enjoy a much clearer view of the interior.

The inside of the skin would be restored to its original condition. Workmen with spray guns that fired liquid nitrogen (temperature: 350 degrees below zero) would blast away the layers of paint, tar, and other materials that had concealed it for so many years. The skin would now shine forth in its original coppery hue.

The visitors would be rewarded when they got to the

top by finding themselves in a newly refurbished observation room. The steel observation platform had rusted and was beginning to rot away. It would be replaced. The rust that had previously scarred the iron framework supporting the head would also be gone—permanently.

The engineers had seriously considered installing an elevator to carry tourists all the way up to the crown, or at least to shoulder height. They regretfully concluded that the limited space inside the Statue made it impossible. It would have required a major rebuilding of Eiffel's interior support framework. That structure had withstood all shocks so well, and was still so remarkably intact, that there was no valid reason for replacing it. A small elevator for emergency and maintenance use was all that could be rigged.

The restoration plans included special consideration for handicapped visitors. The new elevator in the pedestal would be specially designed to give them easier access. Closed-circuit television monitors would be installed in a newly designed colonnade area at the top of the pedestal. The monitors would carry images captured by TV cameras far above in the torch (where visitors are not allowed). The handicapped would be able to enjoy a view of the harbor even more sweeping than the one they would have seen if they had actually made the climb to the crown.

The man most directly responsible for turning all these plans into reality was Angelo Bommarido, foreman of the construction crew. He had a special reason to love his work. "Seventeen years ago I saw the Statue of Liberty at 3 o'clock in the morning," he told *People* magazine in July 1984.

> I was on the boat coming over from Sicily. . . . My mother woke us all up. "*La statua,*" she said. "Look how beautiful it is."
>
> We ran to the deck. The high-class people had rooms above the deck, but we were way down below. . . . I had seen little toy Statues of Liberty, but I never knew how big it was.

Bommarido knew little English when he arrived and worked as a laborer for years. Now he had risen to the rank of foreman, and on this job he was especially serious about his responsibilities. "You gotta be extra careful working on the Statue. There's a lot of history behind it. I try to do the best I can and make sure we do it right. I hope I don't make a boo-boo."

All the elaborate plans that Bommarido and the other workmen were toiling on looked great—on paper. The big question was, how would it all be financed?

13
THE LADY AND HER PEOPLE

There once was a lady from France
Who made Americans' hearts dance.
Though her beauty has faded,
She'll soon be upgraded
If we all chip in and finance.
— Anonymous limerick in the *New York Daily News,* February 1984

As always in the past when the need for funds was urgent, the Statue's guardians looked to the federal government. After all, the Statue had been under federal care and jurisdiction for nearly a hundred years. But on almost every occasion when major funding had been needed previously, the government had turned such requests down. Statue sponsors had to resort to appeals for contributions from the people.

President Ronald Reagan saw no reason to break with this tradition. He could almost certainly have obtained the needed funds from Congress. Public affection and esteem for the Statue had mounted steadily over the years, and there was little doubt that an appropriation of federal funds would have had popular support.

But Reagan's philosophy favored reliance on private enterprise whenever possible. He decided to establish a federal advisory commission consisting of influential private citizens, to raise the funds for the Statue's restoration. As its chairman he appointed Lee A. Iacocca, head of the Chrysler Corporation. Iacocca was well known as one of the nation's most persuasive and forceful business leaders. The commission's membership ranged through broad segments of American society, from a former president of the United Auto Workers to comedian Bob Hope.

The commission was assigned the tasks of restoring not only the Statue, but nearby Ellis Island as well. President Lyndon Johnson had directed that Ellis Island be formally incorporated into the Statue of Liberty National Monument in 1965. Its impressively designed and sturdily constructed buildings, which had once served as the first stop in America for millions of immigrants, had been abandoned since 1954. They were in danger of deteriorating past the point of possible repair.

Lee Iacocca himself was the child of impoverished immigrant parents who had come through Ellis Island. So were several of the other twenty members of his commission. They felt strongly that this historic landmark should not be lost. President Reagan, conscious of his own immigrant ancestry, shared their feeling. He described Ellis Island as "a unifying memory for millions of our citizens."

And so the decision was made to have the former immigrant processing station share in the proceeds of the fund-raising campaign originally intended solely for the Statue. The commission set up the Statue of Liberty-Ellis Island Centennial Foundation to work out every conceivable method for bringing in the amounts needed.

The Ellis Island structures would be adapted for use as a memorial honoring the immigrants. It would house exhibits illustrating their contributions to American life.

How much would all this cost? The commission members considered all the possibilities, took a deep breath, and came up with a daring estimate: $230 million.

That mind-boggling total broke down into four categories. The heaviest expenditure, about $167 million, would go for repair, restoration, and renovation work on the Statue and Ellis Island. As already noted, only some $40 million of that amount was needed for the Lady's beauty treatment. The rest would be spent on the Ellis Island buildings.

Another $20 million would go into an endowment fund, to guarantee future maintenance for both the Statue and Ellis Island. Educational programs and the centennial celebrations (the Statue in 1986, Ellis Island in 1992) would require about $28 million. The remainder, about six and a half percent of the total, would be set aside for administrative and fund-raising expenses.

The campaign would have its official kickoff on the Fourth of July in 1984. The official slogan chosen specifically for the Statue campaign was challenging: "If You Still Believe in Me, Save Me!" Public feeling about the Statue proved so strong that the first preliminary announcement had hardly been made, early in 1983, before donations began to flow in.

The schoolchildren of Bridgeport, Connecticut, collected nearly $3,600. Fifty of the children were taken out to Liberty Island, where they proudly presented their check in person. "The Statue was very big," said one fourth-grader, "and very pretty."

In Tucson, Arizona, the Manzanita elementary school staged a three-mile "Liberty Run." While the more athletic youngsters ran the distance, other students went from door to door canvassing for contribution pledges. They took in $2,400.

Jersey City's Business and Professional Women's Club began collecting what it hoped would amount to tens of thousands of pennies. The campaign's slogan was "Copper pennies for Lady Liberty's copper gown."

On July 4, 1983, twelve athletes ran a twelve-hour "Liberty-to-Liberty" triathlon race. They swam, bicycled, and rowed from the Statue to the Liberty Bell in Philadelphia, a distance of about ninety miles. Each of them was sponsored by a corporation or an individual, who contributed handsomely to the restoration fund.

A more formal fund-raiser was "The Stars Shine for Liberty," an all-star show presented that November at the New York State Theater in New York City's elaborate Lincoln Center complex. Tickets for the show went for as little as $10, but it cost $1,000 to stay for the dinner-dance afterward. When the festivities were over, the Statue had benefited to the tune of over $1 million.

This fund-raising campaign differed dramatically from the long and difficult one of the 1880s. Though all the people, and especially schoolchildren, were once again asked to give whatever they could, there was no problem this time about getting contributions from the rich and powerful. As early as April 1983, fund-raising campaign director I. Paul Bergmoser could announce confidently that $200 million of the needed $230 million would come from about twenty-five of the nation's biggest and best-known corporations.

The foundation offered tempting inducements for businessmen. Advertising and public-relations executives knew that any connection they could establish in the public's mind between their companies and the Statue centennial would have the best possible effect on public opinion. The foundation made such connections easy.

It announced that corporate donors would be permitted to key their organizations' advertising and promotion campaigns to Statue centennial events. In the several TV programs that were planned around the centennial, corporate donors would get "first refusal" on commercial time (that is, they could purchase advertising time on these programs, or refuse it, before anyone else got the chance). And the corporations could use the official Liberty Centennial logo, a sort of postage-stamp-size trademark, in their ads and on company stationery.

Bergmoser told reporters that he planned a direct-mail approach to several million well-to-do households. "The omens are good," he declared. A test mailing of forty thousand requests for funds had drawn a response, with money, from 3.2 percent. "In the direct mail business, a response rate of 0.5 percent is par for the course."

There was another difference between this campaign and that of the previous century. This time, fund-raisers ran into none of the once widepread feeling that the Statue was purely a New York monument, and that its financial problems should therefore be solved by New Yorkers alone. Americans from one end of the country to the other had long since taken the Lady to their hearts. The fund drive of the 1980s was a truly national effort from the outset.

By October 1983, Lee Iacocca was able to announce that several corporations had already pledged a total of $45 million. One of the earliest sponsors was the American Express Company. It announced that from October 1 to the end of the year, the company would contribute

American Express was among the many big corporations that helped finance the restoration.

one cent for every purchase made in the U.S. with an American Express card, and for every purchase of its traveler's checks. Since about a million such transactions took place every day, the company's contribution would amount to about $10,000 a day. Other types of American Express transactions would add another $2,000 a day.

The year 1986 also happened to mark the hundredth birthday of the Coca-Cola company, of Westinghouse, and of Johnson & Johnson. All became major sponsors of the Statue centennial.

Stroh's beer sponsored a five-mile "Run for Liberty" at over a hundred separate locations. Most of the eight-to-ten-dollar registration fee went into the Statue restoration fund. The Kellogg company set up a "Statue of Liberty Honor Roll." In return for two proofs of purchase from any of its cereal boxes, the company would donate 50 cents to the fund; and the names of the purchasers would be published in an Honor Roll in a special edition of *USA Today* on July 4, 1985.

Nestlé offered a $1 donation, plus a medallion of the Statue, plus free entry in a sweepstakes with enticing prizes, for three proofs of purchase. Other big-business supporters included American Airlines, Avon Products, Kodak, Oscar Mayer Foods, International Business Machines, Xerox, and Kimberly-Clark.

The big furniture-moving company, Allied Van Lines, ran a coast-to-coast "Move for Freedom." Allied set up two identical mobile exhibits with photos, artwork, and audiovisual displays relating to the Statue and the history of immigration. One exhibit departed from Washington, D.C., and the other from Seattle on November 1, 1984. They were to visit two hundred cities over the next two years, winding up in New York in time for the centennial celebrations.

At least one famous French company joined the crusade. In October 1984 the makers of Courvoisier cognac announced that they would contribute $5 to the fund for every bottle of their brandy purchased before the end of the year. The total promised to be substantial.

The list of patriotic, fraternal, civic, and labor organizations that joined the drive was even longer than the list of corporations. The Elks, the Freemasons, the Knights of Columbus, the Telephone Pioneers of America, and the Lutheran Aid Association all contributed $1 million or more. Another million pledged by the Disabled American War Veterans was earmarked specifically for work designed to make the Statue more accessible to the handicapped.

Other major gifts came in from the Communications Workers of America, the National Federation of Republican Women, the Daughters of the American Revolution, Amvets, and many more. The list went on and on, a refreshing contrast to the campaign of the 1880s when only one national organization stepped forward to help.

The media too swung into action. One of the first was the *New York Daily News*. It launched a "Save the Lady" drive in February 1984, soliciting contributions from its millions of readers and sponsoring a citywide educational campaign on the history of the Statue and Ellis Island.

In cooperation with the New York City Board of Education, the *News* also ran a contest for elementary- and secondary-school students. They competed with essays, poems, art, and photographic works celebrating America's most famous landmark. The forty-three winners were honored, and received their prizes, in a special ceremony on Liberty Island on June 22, 1984. An unusual feature of the program was the fact that the winners' teachers were also singled out for honors and prizes.

USA Today ran a nationwide poetry contest for schoolchildren, on the theme of liberty. The $2 entry fees swelled the Statue restoration fund. Winners got a trip to New York during the festivities surrounding Liberty's hundredth birthday.

The CBS television network gave the fund drive a big boost with a two-hour "Salute to Lady Liberty" during the Fourth of July weekend in 1984. A dazzling array of movie, stage, and TV stars performed and then made personal appeals for donations to the Statue-Ellis Island fund. Guest star Frank Sinatra, speaking as the son of immigrant parents, explained his lifelong romance with the Lady by describing her as "America's foxiest female." A special segment of the show featured actress Brooke Shields interviewing Bill Gaines, publisher of *Mad* magazine and the nation's most devoted collector of Statue models and memorabilia.

That September, CBS-TV also began broadcasting 130 one-minute spots collectively titled "An American Portrait." The series focused mainly on the achievements of immigrants. Each was narrated by a celebrity. Gregory Peck did the first, which told the story of Emma Lazarus, author of the poem inscribed on the base of the Statue. The series ran until the centennial of the Statue's unveiling on October 28, 1986.

The Advertising Council had a series of skillfully crafted TV spots produced and broadcast on the campaign's behalf. One amusing spot featured the Peanuts comic-strip gang. Another showed several hundred schoolchildren lustily singing "My Country 'Tis of Thee" at the base of the Statue.

The Statue of Liberty-Ellis Island Centennial Foundation itself developed materials and ideas designed to stimulate contributions. It promised to list all donors in an Official Register of Contributors, which would be displayed in the museum at the base of the Statue. Every individual contributor received a handsome certificate acknowledging his or her gift.

The foundation also launched a special "Ancestry Campaign" aimed at the nation's many ethnic minorities. A brochure pointed out that the restoration projects provided "a timely opportunity for all Americans to celebrate their 'roots' and our rich and diverse heritage as a 'Nation of Immigrants.' " The foundation hoped the ethnic groups would contribute more than just money. They were asked to send in oral-history accounts of their members' experiences in the process of becoming Americans, along with suggestions for the use and design of Ellis Island.

But the largest fund-raising plan of all was announced in March 1985. The U.S. Mint was authorized to produce thirty-five and a half million commemorative coins—$5 gold pieces, silver dollars, and 50-cent pieces—to be sold by the government for the Statue-Ellis Island fund. If all of the coins were sold, this promotion alone would bring in no less than $137.5 million.

In April 1985 the space shuttle *Discovery* carried two Statuettes of Liberty cast out of twenty pounds of copper discarded from the skin of the original. One of these fifteen-inch models was then reduced to tens of thousands of commemorative copper seals to be sold through the postal service. The other would be placed on display in the Statue museum.

As the nation's young people moved their fund-raising efforts into high gear, the foundation set up the Liberty Centennial Student Campaign. Lee Iacocca kicked off the campaign with an open letter to schoolchildren. It was published in *Scholastic News* and other school publications in February 1983. The children responded as never before.

Topping all others in the first year of the campaign were the 839 children of the Bauder Elementary School in Seminole, Florida. They learned all they could about the Statue, then built an eight-foot papier-mâché model to stand in the school hallway, and finally held a walkathon which raised $11,700. Running a close second was Madison School No. 1 in Phoenix, Arizona, which collected $11,000.

One of thousands of posters created by schoolchildren for the 1980s fund drive.

The biggest model was probably the one built by students at Altoona Vocational-Technical School, in Pennsylvania. Made of wood, chicken wire, and papier mâché, it stood twenty feet tall. The students had worked on it for two weeks after the school year. They used it not merely to stimulate donations in Altoona; they took it on tour through neighboring communities as well. Their goal of $10,000 was achieved within weeks.

Second-graders in an East Hills, New York, school

enthusiastically explored their own immigrant roots. Each child researched the subject by querying elder family members. The resulting knowledge was painstakingly recorded on a page that went into a book about the student's forebears. Then the class held a bake sale and raffle which raised $440. The children produced some uniquely imaginative posters to advertise their fund-raising effort; one of these is shown on page 187.

An enterprising group of third-graders in Wellston, Oklahoma, took out a $10 loan from a local bank. They bought forty petunia plants. They sold these, bought more, sold and bought still more. After two weeks the children were able to send their tidy profit of $227 to the foundation.

Fifth-graders in Dayton, Ohio, were creative in a different but highly appropriate way. They made and sold copies of an "Ethnic Heritage Cookbook," using recipes supplied by their immigrant grandparents. Then they had the grandparents actually prepare the ethnic dishes. The children sold spoonfuls at a schoolwide "taste-out." Customers got a delectable treat, and the foundation got the profits.

In Richardson, Texas, students at Saint Paul the Apostle School decorated empty ice-cream containers to serve as collection boxes. They handed each donor a hand-drawn, rainbow-colored thank-you card. One of the many posters they spread around town read, "We Don't Want a Leaning Tower of Liberty—Please Donate!" Their total, gathered over a single weekend: $409.

A talent show was the fund-raising method chosen by the boys and girls at the Sacred Heart School in Suffern, New York. It was a smash hit, raising the sum of $1,100. Very nearly matching them was a school in Valley Stream, New York. Its students bought jumbo bags of popcorn, poured them into smaller bags, and sold these in the school cafeteria. They persisted for five months, and raised $1,000. They also wrote to pen-pal schools in Texas and Illinois, and convinced them to do the same.

The Castilleto Middle School, in California's Almaden Valley, held a "Liberty Dance" that raised more than $700. Sixth-graders at the Southwest School in Torrington, Connecticut, set up a toy tag sale. They collected books, games, puzzles, model cars, dolls, audiocassettes and videocassettes, and all sorts of other toys and hobby items. Prices ranged from one cent to $10. They took in over $400.

As the home of the Statue, New York State established its own Centennial Commission and drew up extensive plans for the celebration. The fun started with "Harbor Festival '84," a week-long series of events in New York harbor leading up to the Fourth of July observance. There were women's lifeboat races, yacht races, a "flyby" (parade of aircraft) over the Statue, a fifty-gun salute and roll call of the states, picnics, parades, and, climaxing it all, a tremendous fireworks display.

The state assembly passed a bill in May 1985 that would replace all 9.2 million New York license plates with new ones bearing the Lady's silhouette. Expected to cost some $27 million, this project was to start in 1986 and take about a year. Final passage awaited action by the senate and approval by Governor Mario Cuomo.

Centennial parades were arranged in about nine hundred New York cities and towns. The biggest of these, a "Worldwide Unity Parade," was set to march in New York City on the Fourth of July, 1986. As headquarters for the United Nations, New York also arranged for members of that organization to set up an international "Salute to the Statue of Liberty."

A special role was laid out for one of New York's largest trade unions, the International Ladies Garment Workers Union. Largely composed of immigrants and the children of immigrants ever since its formation in the 1880s, the ILGWU planned a "Pilot Centennial" program that served as a model for other unions. The program would highlight the Americanization process as the union's members had actually lived it.

New York's Centennial Commission made a special arrangement with the widely acclaimed French-born sculptor known only as Erté. He created a modernized bronze version of "Liberty, Fearless and Free." A limited edition of five hundred copies, each about two feet high, was cast from his original. Erté pledged to donate most of the profits, expected to amount to about $350,000, to the Statue restoration fund.

With so many trying so hard in so many ways and in so many places from coast to coast, the results gave the entire nation cause for pride. By March 1985, with nearly a year and a half of fund raising still ahead, the foundation had collected nearly $145 million. About three-fourths had come from corporations and other organizations, and one-fourth from individuals. Schoolchildren alone had raised about $1.4 million.

America's love affair with the Lady has brought her people together in joy, generosity, and sheer unembarrassed patriotism.

· 14 ·

BELOVED LADY

She has a soul of her own–strong, caring. She speaks to people in a silent language, universal– everyone understands. She speaks of what people have been fighting for for hundreds of years. . . . The Statue's a shrine.

— Charlie DeLeo, Statue of Liberty maintenance mechanic, 1984

So many have loved her. They have come to her from every class and from every land. These have been some of her lovers:

• over a hundred thousand French men, women, and children, who gave their hard-earned francs to build her;

• descendants of American Revolution soldiers, both French and American, who revered her as a memorial to the shared struggle;

• Civil War veterans of the Union army, who saw in her a fitting tribute to their historic victory;

• over one hundred twenty thousand Americans of all ages, whose pennies and dimes and dollars built her a pedestal worthy of her nobility;

• millions of immigrants, whose hearts have been uplifted by her torch-lit welcome;

• tens of thousands of American fighting men, whom the Lady has saluted on their way overseas and on their return;

• ever-increasing millions of visitors, who throng to her from every state in the nation and every country in the world;

• generations of refugees, fleeing every kind of tyranny;

• women's-rights advocates, who claim her as a personification of female pride, independence, and idealism;

• executives of giant American corporations, members of patriotic, civic, fraternal, and labor organizations, thousands of private citizens, and many more schoolchildren, who piled up millions of dollars in the mid-1980s to repair her storm-lashed form and restore her to unsullied beauty in time for her hundredth birthday;

• people in every part of the planet, whose dream of freedom and a better life she embodies.

Miss Liberty's people have worked out an almost infinite variety of ways to express their affection.

Consider, for example, the case of Ermenegildo Meneschi. He first saw the Lady when he arrived in the United States around 1900. Meneschi was so profoundly moved that he made a vow to visit her every year, on his birthday. He was there as always, smiling through the tears, on his hundredth birthday in 1979.

Joe Hydrusko's story is different. He was a sailor on a U.S. Navy hospital ship stationed at Pearl Harbor, Hawaii, on December 7, 1941. Throughout the sneak attack by Japanese bombers that morning, Hydrusko led a group of sailors on repeated rescue missions in a small boat out among the burning and sunken ships of the U.S. Pacific Fleet. His heroism saved more than three hundred wounded and often drowning Americans, including twenty-four men trapped in the capsized battleship *Oklahoma*. The Navy later awarded Hydrusko a plaque and a special decoration.

For years afterward, Hydrusko looked for some suitable way to commemorate that "day of infamy." Hawaii was too far for an annual excursion from his home in Massapequa, New York. In 1969, at the age of fifty, he became a licensed pilot. And then he got a terrific idea. Why not create a ceremony that could be shared with the Lady he loved? On December 7 of each year after that, Hydrusko flew over the Statue and dropped roses in honor of those shipmates who never came home.

Hydrusko died in July 1983, after his plane exploded while being readied for takeoff. A group of pilot friends pledged to carry on the tradition he had created. On December 7, 1984, eleven planes made the pilgrimage. Ten of them flew in formation above the Statue while the eleventh swooped low. Then Mike Savarese, one of the sailors Hydrusko had pulled from the *Oklahoma,* leaned out and dropped forty-three red roses—one for each year since Pearl Harbor—and one pink one in memory of Joe Hydrusko.

Even the people of faraway lands have found ways to demonstrate what the Lady means to them. A unique example is a beautiful silk rug, about six feet by ten feet, hand-woven by Armenian craftsmen in Siraz, Turkey, in 1890. It is a portrait of the Statue, and the loving effort lavished on it is obvious to all who view it. An Armenian immigrant brought the treasured rug with him when he immigrated to America. It is now on display in the museum in the base of the Statue.

Viktoria Mullova came from an equally distant homeland. This attractive young Soviet-born concert violinist defected to the United States in 1983. Her American business manager met her at LaGuardia Airport. He thought a quick tour of New York City might be a pleasant way to introduce her to her adopted country. He drove down Fifth Avenue, pointing out all the high-fashion shops: Gucci, Saks, Cartier, etc. Her response was blank. She had never heard of them.

Then he took her down to the Battery and pointed out the Statue. She reacted instantly. "Stop the car!" she yelled. At last, he had found for her one of the very few American landmarks that even Soviet citizens admire. Mullova insisted on having her picture taken with the Statue in the background. Only then did she begin to feel at home in America.

Lady Liberty herself has been made to feel at home by the steady rise in the number of her visitors. A few random dates will make the point. On August 8, 1894, exactly sixty-nine Americans from eleven states signed the guest book. There were also twelve visitors from eight foreign countries. On the same date forty years later in 1934, over twelve hundred tourists registered from thirty-six states and twenty-five foreign lands. The Lady was then receiving a total of about two hundred fifty thousand guests a year. That number had doubled by the end of World War II in 1945. The total reached one million in 1971. Today, even that stupendous figure has doubled.

The Lady's guests have left some poignant impressions. A crewman on the ferry that brings them over from Manhattan was asked if the visitors show any emotion. "Well," he replied, "I've seen them kiss the ground."

David L. Moffitt, superintendent of the Statue, told a reporter for the Long Island newspaper *Newsday* about an incident that touched him deeply:

> Once, I was climbing the stairs [inside the Statue] behind a visitor, a bit impatient at his slow pace. When I got to the crown, I saw that the man was blind. From that moment on, I realized that people climb the Statue of Liberty for more than the view.

One cold winter morning during World War II, the first ferry brought only one visitor, a young woman. She seemed pale and shaky. One of the National Park Service Rangers on duty asked if she needed any help. She told him that her soldier-husband had just been sent overseas. "I've been waiting since early morning for the ferry to bring me here. I just wanted to remind myself why he had to go."

A World War II soldier of the First Armored Division had been captured by the Germans. One of the guards kept taunting him, repeating over and over again that he'd never see the Statue of Liberty again. Liberated at the war's end and back with his old outfit, the former P.O.W. stayed up all night to see the Statue as his troopship steamed into New York harbor. "This is the day," he told his buddies with a long sigh, "that we've been dreaming about for three and a half years."

Another GI returning from the war greeted the Lady affectionately: "Take down your torch, honey. I'm home!"

In a letter to the author, Thomas J. Smith, Jr., of Galveston, Texas, spoke for many of the veterans:

> I shall never forget the day we sailed out of New York harbor in July 1942 for foreign duty . . . and watched as the Great Lady faded into the distance. For each of us it meant another kind of future, unknown, and [filled] with great apprehension.

Soon after he got back, Smith made the trip to New York and "climbed the Statue to really feel what it was like to be a part of her makeup. It was a thrill that I shall never forget."

New York's Seventy-seventh Division has had a special relationship with the Lady ever since the division was organized in 1917. This outfit, veteran of battle on many fronts, is the "Liberty Division." Its men and women wear an image of the Statue as their official insignia.

The Lady also has a special meaning for men of the sea. Captain Sir Arthur Rostron first gained fame as master of the British ship *Carpathia,* which rescued many survivors of the supposedly unsinkable luxury liner *Titanic* way back in 1912. He subsequently had a long and distinguished maritime career. Captain Rostron had thought about the Lady a great deal:

> She's in a class by herself. Sailors have a real affection for her. She often reminds me of a mother—the mother of the universe—holding aloft her light to lead the lost world to her feet.

Louis B. Evans of Delaware was a captain and pilot in New York harbor for forty years. "That Statue of Liberty always meant a lot to me," he wrote to a reporter for *GEO* magazine.

> I brought many a transport ship into the harbor with crippled servicemen. . . . It sometimes broke me down, and I had to compose myself before docking the ship. But how they cheered coming into that harbor!

Men who have worked on the Lady, repairing the ravages of time and weather, develop a deep affection for her. Bob Conmy helped erect the huge aluminum scaffolding that encaged the Statue during the major restoration effort in the mid-1980s. Conmy told a *New York Times* reporter that he "was one of the first people in 98 years to look her right in the two-and-a-half-foot eye." As soon as he got close enough, he gave the Lady a big kiss.

An electrician working on the same project said, "There is no need for supervision. This is something you want to do. She is all ours for a while."

The feelings of these usually hard-boiled workmen were perhaps summed up best by Joe Fiebiger: "I guess, whether we admit it or not, we are all in love with her, for different reasons. I don't want to sound foolish. I am a blacksmith."

Most of the Lady's admirers are content just knowing she's out there, but there are some who feel a need to surround themselves with mementos of her. Outstanding among the latter are Bill Gaines, publisher of *Mad* magazine, and his companion, Anne Griffiths. These two have filled their New York City home with the world's largest private collection of Statue models and memorabilia.

Gaines has loved the Statue for as long as he can remember. He and Griffiths were visiting it one day, toward evening, in 1977. They persuaded the officials to allow them to climb up through the arm to the little balcony around the torch, which has been closed to the public since 1916. Griffiths was so thrilled that, in her own words, she "fell in love" and became a Statue devotee.

Soon afterward, a bronze miniature that had been cast

from one of the original models created by Bartholdi was offered for sale at an auction. Gaines bought it for Griffiths, and that was the start of their obsession. "We just started picking up everything we could find," Gaines told the author, "and all our friends and relatives started giving us presents. Pretty soon we had a very large collection."

It now ranges from a steel model nearly seven feet high built in the United States in 1918, to a magnificent gold and silver miniature about a foot high. The latter was fabricated by Tiffany & Co., the famous American jewelers, and was presented to a French general as a gift from the American people during World War I. Gaines and Griffiths have even brought together dozens of pieces of silverware, mostly spoons, with the Statue worked into the handles.

Theirs is an expensive hobby. In December 1984 a very rare four-foot model was put up for auction in New York. Made of zinc alloy electroplated with copper to simulate bronze, it was one of only six cast by the sculptor in the early 1880s to raise funds for the building of the Statue. The seller was a European who had acquired it in South America, of all places. Gaines outbid all rivals and purchased it—at a cost of a whopping $104,500 plus $8,500 in taxes.

Equally dedicated are the New Jersey-born Eger brothers, Dick and Jeffrey, both in their thirties. Dick has amassed some five hundred picture postcards, World War I song sheets, and old-time advertising cards, all featuring the Statue. Jeffrey owns an unrivaled collection of postage stamps and books on the monument's history.

Statue admirers in many parts of the U.S. and several other countries have shown their esteem by building large replicas. None of these is nearly as large as the colossus itself, however.

There are two in Paris. One of them is one-fourth the size of the original. It stands on an island in the Seine River, not far from the Eiffel Tower. Americans living in Paris gave it to the city in 1884. The other Paris copy is somewhat smaller; it graces the famous Luxembourg Gardens.

The Statue itself was still brand new when the French built yet another model in far-off Hanoi, second largest city of what was then French Indo-China (now Vietnam). This carefully detailed copy served as the centerpiece of a world's fair that France staged in her Indo-China colony in 1887. It remained one of the city's favorite sights until it disappeared in 1945, a time of great upheaval in that part of the world.

More unexpected is the fact that models of the Statue have been set up in both of the Japanese cities ravaged by the atomic bomb at the end of World War II. The city of Hiroshima erected one near its devastated center in 1947, as a symbol of peace. The fifteen-inch bronze copy in Nagasaki was a 1951 gift from a group of American businessmen.

The largest model ever built anywhere stands atop a warehouse on the upper west side of Manhattan, in New York City. The warehouse owner, William H. Flattau, was a prosperous Russian immigrant who wished to express his gratitude to his new country. He had the Statue copy erected in 1902. About one-third the size of the original, it towers fifty-five feet above its pedestal. It was made in Pennsylvania of quarter-inch steel, and is maintained in gleaming condition under a coat of silver paint.

Another large likeness, five stories high, stood in Times

Square, New York City, during World War II, but this one was only a temporary model made of white asbestos. It promoted the sale of War Bonds. The lights in its torch were turned on from the White House in Washington when President Franklin D. Roosevelt touched a switch on November 11, 1944. A steady stream of popular entertainers and bands performed on two stages in front of the replica, keeping the public beguiled–and buying bonds. Millions of dollars' worth were sold.

A much smaller but extremely attractive copy of the Statue stands on the grounds of the Texas state capitol at Austin. The five-foot bronze was a gift to the state from the Boy Scouts.

Schoolchildren built several models of impressive size during the great fund-raising campaign of the mid-1980s. This was only one of their astonishingly varied activities on behalf of the fund for the Statue's repair and restoration, prior to its centennial. But these were never meant to outlast the campaign.

Many American business concerns include the world "liberty" in their names, and some also use an image of the Statue in their logos or trademarks. Prominent among these is the Liberty National Life Insurance Company. Its management had a thirty-one-foot bronze replica fabricated in France in 1958. The handsome likeness now adorns the company headquarters in Birmingham, Alabama.

Chemical Bank owns a four-foot model in white metal, cast by the French firm of Avoiron et Clément in the 1880s under Bartholdi's supervision. This model originally belonged to the now defunct Liberty National Bank of New York. Chemical had it specially repaired and refurbished for display at the bank's New York headquarters during the 1985–86 celebration of the hun-

One of the biggest models of the Statue ever built helped sell War Bonds in Times Square, New York, during World War II.

dredth anniversary of the Statue's unveiling. The bank also maintains an archive of historical materials relating to the Statue, and employs a full-time professional archivist to assist scholars with research projects pertaining to it.

Columbia Pictures, one of the nation's oldest motion-picture producers and distributors, has long used a variant of the Statue image as its logo. Movie fans and TV viewers will doubtless recall its photographic depiction of a stately and attractive woman, draped in a style similar to the Lady's but rather more revealing, and holding a torch on high.

Exploitation of the Statue for business purposes is nothing new. From the time she was built until the present, businessmen have sought ways to profit from the Lady's popularity. Corporations of all sorts have appropriated the monument for use in advertising and publicity materials of every imaginable description.

Just scan any newspaper or magazine, look around a railroad or bus station or airport, observe the billboards on any highway, or watch the TV commercials. The Statue ranks among the most frequently used—and abused—images in all media. Perhaps the most common such abuse has been to show the Lady holding up some product, or a sign bearing the product's name or trademark, in place of her torch.

An amusing example cropped up in the ads for the 1984 movie *Supergirl.* Since some of the film's action occurs around the Statue, the ads featured a drawing of the monument—but the Lady was shown with the torch in her left hand.

This was by no means the first time the Statue had played a role in a movie. Filmmakers have been taking advantage of the monument's worldwide familiarity for years. Movies featuring it have included Alfred Hitchcock's classic suspense thriller *Saboteur* (1942), the science-fiction adventure *Planet of the Apes* (1967), the Barbra Streisand spectacular *Funny Girl* (1968), and the comedy *Splash* (1984), as well as *Supergirl.*

Of course the Lady also appears constantly in advertising or promotions of a patriotic or public-service nature. When the cause is good, she is content to lend it her prestige.

Not surprisingly, Miss Liberty has also been honored in that fascinating medium through which nations demonstrate their special regard for select people, places, and historic objects—postage stamps.

The first Statue of Liberty stamp was a U.S. fifteen-cent issue printed in 1922. Perhaps the most appropriate stamp featuring the Statue was one that appeared in 1943. It honored the "Four Freedoms," President Franklin D. Roosevelt's famous summing-up of the Allies' war aims in World War II. As stated on the "first-day cover" which accompanied the publication of this stamp, its purpose was "to emphasize the necessity of world-wide freedom of speech, freedom of religion, freedom from want and freedom from fear."

A similar theme was stated in a 1975 issue (reprinted in 1981), which paid tribute to "Freedom of Conscience—An American Right."

A 1978 stamp celebrated the Statue's special meaning as a symbol of welcome for millions of immigrants. It highlighted the Lady's head and bore the familiar concluding line from "The New Colossus," Emma Lazarus's poem about the Statue: "I Lift My Lamp Beside the Golden Door."

Special care went into the planning for the commemorative stamp honoring the Statue's 1986 centennial.

The Statue became the symbol of President Franklin D. Roosevelt's "Four Freedoms" in 1943.

A total of thirty-five other countries too have memorialized the Lady in 140 different stamps. France, her birthplace, was one of the first to do so. The French brought out a noteworthy issue on the Statue's fiftieth anniversary in 1936. This stamp honored the concept of aid to refugees, a timely theme in that ominous prewar period when thousands of European victims of persecution had to flee their native lands. It bore a portrait of the Lady in which the date on the tablet cradled in her left arm (July 4, 1776) was replaced by the hopeful word *Fraternité* ("Brotherhood").

Spain, Argentina, Uruguay, Peru, and Liberia are among the other nations that have featured the Statue in stamps. Even a communist country, Bulgaria, has paid homage to the Lady. The occasion was the 1959 visit of Nikita Khrushchev, then head of the Soviet government, to the United States. The stamp visualized his journey as an attempt to bridge the gap between the two countries by showing the Kremlin, the Statue, and a tiny airliner flying between them.

This love affair between so many people in so many lands and a colossal copper-skinned Lady with a lamp has been a long one. It has not always run smooth.

The Lady began winning hearts from the moment she was conceived. First she had to overcome the natural skepticism of the French people. Then she had the even more formidable task of captivating the tough-minded Americans. And then there remained the people of the world. Some have succumbed to her charms. Others have rebuffed her.

The Lady stands her ground. She holds her torch on high for all who need the light of liberty. New lovers come to her every day.

· 15 ·
THE LADY'S ETERNAL MYSTERY

To countless millions, [the Statue's] real significance was always the next freedom, the needed freedom, that which as yet had not even been expressed. . . .

— Herta Pauli and E.B. Ashton, *I Lift My Lamp: The Way of a Symbol,* 1948

What does the Statue of Liberty *mean*? The answer is not as obvious as it may seem.

Over the century of her existence, the Lady has acquired a whole complex of meanings. People of different periods have seen in her what they needed to see. They have interpreted her in ways that reflected the attitudes and problems of their times. The Lady has loomed large enough to carry several meanings at once.

We have seen how Lady Liberty started life as an almost mystical dream harbored by a small group of freedom-loving Frenchmen. Their leader, Edouard de Laboulaye, conceived the notion of a monument commemorating the French-American alliance that ensured victory in the American Revolution. The monument would be built jointly by the people of both nations. Laboulaye and his friends hoped the campaign to raise funds for it would promote republican sentiment in the autocratic France of Emperor Napoleon III.

Then Bartholdi brought the idea to America, and it began to change. Americans were naturally flattered by the gift, with its tribute to the United States as a shining model of democracy triumphant over tyranny. For some, however, the memory of the recent Civil War was more alive than the Revolution. Those who had fought to preserve the Union and abolish slavery felt that the real meaning of the proposed monument was to honor their cause.

Thus the campaigns to finance the Statue and its pedestal got under way in France and the United States with very different motivations. Each nation saw the Statue through the prism of its own history, its own politics, its own national character.

Through the ensuing century, the two peoples maintained a special friendship and a steadfast alliance, despite occasional moments of mutual irritation. The celebrations surrounding the Statue's centennial renewed and revitalized their relationship.

A great French-American "cultural festival" marked the occasion. It had first been proposed by Jack Lang, France's cultural envoy, during a visit to the United States in November 1984. France, Lang said, "would be honored to welcome and acclaim some of the finest American [artistic] companies." In return, French artists would be sent to the United States "to bear witness through their creative accomplishments that the spirit of liberty, our greatest wealth, continues to thrive in old Europe as it inspires the New World."

Lang's proposal was warmly welcomed by American

cultural leaders. They set to work immediately, working with the French authorities to plan a brilliant program of exchanges of exhibitions and performances in every branch of the arts. With her dual citizenship, the Lady was of course the spiritual guest of honor at all of these festivities. Her meaning for the cause of international friendship had never shone with a brighter luster.

But she had a long way to go before that happy occasion could even be dreamed of. Back in the 1880s, when the fund drive for the pedestal was starting on its difficult course in America, the country was changing. New tides of immigration were sweeping in. These were partly the result of renewed persecutions of Jews in Russia, and partly the result of deepening poverty among the peoples of southern and eastern Europe.

The changes in American life were mirrored in the work of the young poet Emma Lazarus. She was asked to contribute a poem to an auction for the benefit of the pedestal fund. Her ardent sonnet, "The New Colossus," was virtually ignored at first. Over the years it captured the affection of America, and eventually of the world. It transformed the public's perception of the Statue. The Lady with her upraised torch was seen as a herald of welcome for the world's "huddled masses yearning to breathe free."

Meanwhile, America went right on changing. Long isolated from international conflicts, the United States was increasingly involved in world affairs. World War I broke out in 1914. Despite all efforts to remain neutral, America was drawn into the war in 1917.

The people of France welcomed the arriving American troops with wild enthusiasm. The representatives of liberty in the New World had come to the rescue of its hard-pressed defenders in the Old. America was repaying the ancient debt to her ally of Revolutionary days.

The meaning of American entry into the war was fittingly symbolized when an American delegation presented a foot-high gold and silver model of the Statue to the commander of France's armies, Marshal Joseph Joffre. The *New York World* had raised the needed funds. The model is now one of the most valuable items in the collection of Statue miniatures owned by Bill Gaines and Anne Griffiths.

As America's war effort intensified, the Statue began to acquire an all-encompassing new image.

The war required immense new expenditures. The government had to turn to the people for funds. It planned a series of War Bond drives. A symbol was needed to express the spirit of America and the ideals underlying its war effort. President Wilson had declared that our sole purpose in entering the war was "to make the world safe for democracy." America sought no advantage for itself, no new conquests or territories.

The Statue was perfectly suited to this idealistic spirit. The War Bonds became Liberty Bonds. The Lady appeared in posters, billboards, and advertisements that blanketed the country, appealing to the people's patriotism and generosity. Americans responded by buying an awesome total of $15 billion worth of Liberty Bonds. That amounted to about half the entire cost of the war.

In the process of achieving this phenomenal popular success, the Statue came to signify much more than any one aspect of the American experience. It still incorporated all its previously accepted meanings—revolution, independence, freedom, French-American friendship, preservation of the Union, abolition of slavery, welcome for the world's oppressed. But in the popular imagination the monument now seemed to express something

For every generation, a new meaning.

that transcended all of these: America itself, America at its best.

America had other symbols. Above all there was the flag, with all the rich imagery implied in its stars and stripes. There was also the American eagle, which the Founding Fathers had chosen during the Revolution as the emblem of the new nation.

The Statue was, and is, different. Its origins, its history, its physical form, its spiritual essence say things about America that go so deep they can be expressed in no other way. Ever since World War I, this French-born Lady has stood forth as the ultimate embodiment of the American dream.

Her ideals were soon to face their gravest challenge. In the 1920s and 1930s, new political and social systems arose in Europe. Communism triumphed in Russia. Fascism came to power in Italy, and Nazism in Germany. These totalitarian forms of goverment produced new waves of political and religious refugees. Many of them emigrated to the United States.

Among the new immigrants were some of the world's most distinguished figures in the arts, sciences, humanities, and medicine. They vastly enriched America's cultural life.

Understandably, these refugees were deeply concerned about the rising threat of totalitarianism. As they came through the gateway of the Narrows into New York harbor, they perceived the Statue differently from those who had preceded them. For them it represented America as an endangered fortress, holding aloft the torch of freedom in a world menaced by ever more powerful forces of oppression. The refugees did all they could to arouse Americans to the danger.

President Franklin D. Roosevelt was one of the first to comprehend the peril. In January 1941, when World War II was going very badly for the Allies but the United States was not yet engaged, he gave eloquent voice to the aspirations of mankind. The postwar world, said Roosevelt, must be founded on "four essential human freedoms." These were "freedom of speech and expression . . . freedom of every person to worship God in his own way . . . freedom from want . . . [and] freedom from fear."

Ever since, the anniversary of Roosevelt's Four Freedoms speech has been an occasion for celebration. It has seemed entirely natural and inevitable that an image of the Statue would become a central feature of these observances. The Lady is often the focus of Four Freedoms posters, and either she or her torch has been featured on Four Freedoms postage stamps.

As a female, the Lady has inevitably attracted special attention from women. Suffragettes (women campaigning for the right to vote) endowed her with a new meaning as their champion, starting with their first demonstration during the dedication ceremonies in 1886.

Thirty years later, when Congress was voting funds for a new lighting system, a prominent suffragette named Elizabeth Selden Rogers wrote an angry letter to the *New York Times.* She denounced Congress for appropriating money for the Statue while refusing to pass an amendment to the Constitution guaranteeing women the right to vote. Only when it was passed, she wrote, "will the Statue of Liberty be lighted by the glow of truth. Until then let this hypocritical talk of liberty cease."

Elizabeth Selden Rogers did not have long to wait. In

1920 the Nineteenth Amendment gave women the right to vote. Liberty's light glowed that much more brightly.

Starting in the 1960s, many women became active in new campaigns for women's rights. They insisted that women were kept in a social and economic status inferior to that of men, and they demanded equality. Once again the struggle centered on a constitutional amendment, the so-called Equal Rights Amendment.

These activists have claimed the Lady for their cause. They see her as their heroic ideal: positive, self-assured, independent, with tremendous inner strength—all qualities admired by feminists. They have dramatized their crusade by staging demonstrations on Liberty Island, even occupying the Statue on at least one occasion.

Ironically, it was the two world wars that endowed the Statue with still another meaning: Lady of Peace. This development was first foreshadowed in President Woodrow Wilson's 1916 statement, at the banquet celebrating the Statue's new lighting system, that "peace is going to come to the world only through Liberty." Very much on Wilson's mind as he spoke was the bloody and seemingly endless slaughter of World War I, which was then at its height.

The peace theme was taken up again shortly after World War II. On August 11, 1947, officials of the city of Hiroshima, Japan, announced a plan to build a replica of the Statue. It would be placed on the site of a castle near the city's center, which had been obliterated by the atomic bomb. Hiroshima's own citizens would pay the cost. Erection of the Statue replica was to be part of the rehabilitation of the city, which was still largely in ruins.

These victims of the first wartime use of the atomic bomb had voted to dedicate their devastated city to the cause of world peace. In the spirit of Woodrow Wilson, they enshrined the Statue as a reminder to all mankind that peace could triumph only in a world enlightened by liberty. Every year since then, on the August 6 anniversary of the bombing of Hiroshima, the memorial ceremonies have included homage to Japan's own Lady.

Nagasaki, second Japanese city to be ravaged by the A-bomb, has acquired its own model of the Statue. In 1952 a group of American businessmen sent a handsome fifteen-inch bronze miniature as a gift to the mayor of Nagasaki. It occupies a central position today in the Nagasaki Peace Center.

A 1960 article by historian Richard B. Morris in the *New York Times Magazine* argued for the adoption of the Statue not only as a token of peace, but as America's national symbol. Morris challenged the traditional use of the bald eagle to represent the nation: "Do we want America to be symbolized abroad by an emblem of imperial might, rapacity, and brute power?"

In place of the eagle Morris urged adoption of "that inspired colossus," the Statue of Liberty. Bartholdi's creation, Morris declared, "stands for peace through freedom rather than peace through subjugation. . . . Let us by our emblem demonstrate that we bring not the sword of enslavement but the torch of liberty. . . ."

Morris's proposal has never been formally adopted. It seems doubtful that any law will ever be passed making the Statue the official national symbol of the United States. But such a law is probably unnecessary.

The Lady has been working out her own meaning in the minds and hearts of Americans—and of people all over the world—ever since her creation. In those dark times when America has been shaken by doubts about herself, when fear or bigotry has turned Americans against one another, the Lady has been depicted as weeping. But when America has boldly lived her destiny as the land of the Four Freedoms, the Lady's ultimate meaning has been plain to all.

She represents America. She represents America at her most courageous, her most compassionate. She represents the America that Abraham Lincoln called "the last, best hope of earth."

She represents a dream. She represents mankind's oldest dream. She represents the dream of being free, of living at peace, of becoming truly human.

And yet there still persists a tantalizing mystery about the Lady. What will she mean to the people of the future? We can scarcely conceive of the new interpretations that tomorrow's humanity may find for her, just as her original creators could hardly have imagined her multiple meanings of today. All we can venture to predict is that the Lady will mean what generations yet unborn will need her to mean.

There is also the dire possibility of another future for the Lady. One place in which it was sketched out was a highly imaginative novel of the 1960s called *The Planet of the Apes,* which became a popular movie.

It tells of a group of American astronauts who travel through time, far into the future. They find themselves in a world ruled by highly evolved apes, where human beings have degenerated into a despised, degraded, enslaved species. Perplexed as to how this horror came about, the astronauts discover the shattered remnants of the Statue, washed up onto a deserted beach.

The grim truth is instantly clear to them. While they were hurtling through the time barrier, human civilization, symbolized by the Statue, had destroyed itself in a nuclear war.

But that was merely fiction. We can prevent it from becoming reality.

The Lady still stands. She still holds aloft her beacon of hope. She may yet light our way to joyous tomorrows.

SUGGESTIONS FOR FURTHER READING

BOOKS

Bell, James B., and Richard I. Abrams. *In Search of Liberty: The Story of the Statue of Liberty and Ellis Island.* Garden City, New York: Doubleday, 1984. A large-size, lavishly illustrated paperback, with concise text.

Blanchet, Christian, and Bertrand Dard. *The Statue of Liberty.* English text by Bernard Weisberger, adapted from the French original. New York: American Heritage, 1985. A deluxe volume, richly illustrated.

George, Michael. *The Statue of Liberty.* New York: Abrams, 1985. Thirty oversize photographs, with brief text by the photographer.

Handlin, Oscar. *Statue of Liberty.* New York: Newsweek, 1971. A distinguished historian tells the story. Includes a set of excerpts from primary sources.

Kroske, Robert. *The Statue of Liberty Comes to America.* New York: Garrard, 1972. For younger children.

Levine, Benjamin, and I. F. Story. *Statue of Liberty National Monument.* Washington, D.C.: National Park Service, 1975. The U.S. Government's official, fact-filled pamphlet.

Mercer, Charles. *Statue of Liberty.* New York: Putnam, 1979. For younger children.

Merriam, Eve. *Emma Lazarus: Woman with a Torch.* New York: Citadel Press, 1956. A moving and insightful biography.

———. *The Voice of Liberty.* New York: Farrar, Strauss & Cudahy and Jewish Publications Inc., 1959. Fictionalized biography, for young readers.

Nash, Margo. *Statue of Liberty: Keeper of Dreams.* New York: Berry Enterprises, 1983. Another big, well-illustrated paperback.

Pauli, Herta, and E. B. Ashton. *I Lift My Lamp: The Way of a Symbol.* New York: Appleton-Century-Crofts, 1948 (reprinted, Port Washington, New York: Friedman, 1968). Thoughtful approach to the Statue's history.

Schappes, Morris U., ed. *Emma Lazarus: Selections from Her Poetry and Prose.* 5th ed. New York: Emma Lazarus Federation, 1982. An impressive sampling, with a concise biography that fleshes out the historical context. Paperback.

Swanberg, W. A. *Pulitzer.* New York: Charles Scribner's Sons, 1967. A lively and sympathetic biography.

Trachtenberg, Marvin. *Statue of Liberty.* New York: Viking, 1976. Analysis of the Statue's origins and merit as a work of art.

Vogel, Dan. *Emma Lazarus.* Boston: Twayne Publishers, 1980. Critical biography by a literary scholar.

Weinbaum, Paul. *Statue of Liberty: Heritage of America.* Las Vegas, Nevada: KC Publications, 1979. Still another outsize, colorful paperback.

PERIODICALS

Edward, C. "The Unveiling of a Great Lady." *American History Illustrated,* February 1979. Fascinating account of an exciting day.

Fleming, Thomas. "Save the Statue of Liberty!" *Readers Digest,* July 1983. A rousing plea for contributions to the Statue's repair and restoration.

Golden, Frederic. "Lady in a Cage." *Discover,* July 1984. Describes the restoration plan.

Heidish, Marcy. "The Grande Dame of the Harbor." *GEO,* July 1984. Features interviews with workmen repairing the Statue.

"Torch Song: A Photographer Angles In on the Statue of Liberty." *LIFE,* March 1983. Captivating and unusual photos.

Morris, Richard B. "Is the Eagle Un-American?" *New York Times Magazine,* February 14, 1960. Historian proposes adoption of the Statue as the U.S. national symbol.

Russell, John. "A Face That Really Launched 1,000 Ships—and Many More." *Smithsonian,* July 1984. Chief art critic of the *New York Times* discusses the Statue's lasting significance.

PICTURE CREDITS

National Park Service, Statue of Liberty National Monument: Pages 3, 14, 31, 35, 50, 65, 68, 123, 170, 201, 210.

Musée Bartholdi, Colmar, France: Pages 11(2), 23(2), 25.

Chemical Bank Archives: Pages 113, 120, 129, 204.

Museum of the City of New York: Pages 85, 99.

Rare Book Division, New York Public Library; Astor, Lenox and Tilden Foundations: Pages 36–37, 40.

American Express Travel Related Services Company, Inc.: Page 182.

Author: Page 164.

Martha Harris: Page 187.

Paul Nadar: Page 29.

Newsday: Pages 160–161.

J. L. Snyder–U.S. Coast Guard: Page 167.

Wide World Photos: Pages 154–155.

INDEX